RELENTLESS

A RENAISSANCE THEOLOGY
FOR THE 21st CENTURY CHURCH

Tom Rawls

INTEGRITY
MEDIA EUROPE

Integrity Media Europe
Unit 1 Hargreaves Business Park
Hargreaves Road
Eastbourne
BN23 6QW

www.worshipwithintegrity.com
www.iworship24-7.com

Copyright © Tom Rawls 2010

All rights reserved. No part of this publication may be reproduced, stored in a retrieval system, or transmitted in any form or by any means, electronic, mechanical, photocopying or otherwise, without the prior written consent of the publisher. Short extracts may be used for review purposes.

Unless otherwise stated, all Scripture quotations are taken from the Holy Bible, New International Version. Copyright © 1973, 1978, 1984 by Biblica

AMP – The Amplified Bible. Copyright © 1954, 1958, 1962, 1964, 1965, 1987 by The Lockman Foundation

MSG – The Message. Copyright © 1993, 1994, 1995, 1996, 2000, 2001, 2002 by Eugene H. Peterson

NKJV – The Holy Bible, New King James Version. Copyright © 1982 by Thomas Nelson Inc.

KJV – The Holy Bible, King James Version. Public domain.

ISBN 978-1-907080-16-6

Cover art by Liz Morgan
Photo of Tom Rawls by Daniel Hills
Typeset by Richard Weaver
Printed in Malta

Contents

What Others Are Saying About *Relentless* — 5
Dedication — 14
Acknowledgements — 15
Foreword — 16
Preface — 18
Introduction — 25

PART ONE – A Renaissance of Leadership and Understanding the Centrality of the Church

- Chapter 1 Something is Broken — 37
- Chapter 2 Fixing the Problem — 53
- Chapter 3 Becoming an Expert Builder — 71
- Chapter 4 A Church in Your City — 85
- Chapter 5 What Do You Really Believe — 99
- Chapter 6 The Centrality of the Church — 111
- Chapter 7 The Impact and Focus of the Church — 121

PART TWO – A Renaissance of Key Values

- Chapter 8 Who's Building Whose Church? — 137
- Chapter 9 The House of God – Restoring Key Values — 151
- Chapter 10 Finding Meaning and Function — 161

PART THREE – The 7 Characteristics of a 21st Century *Relentless* Church

- Chapter 11 Relentless Church – Revivalist, Prophetic, Evangelistic — 177
- Chapter 12 Relentless Church – Connected, Salvation-orientated, Spiritual, Contemporary — 187

PART FOUR – Rediscovering Jesus

- Chapter 13 Jesus – The Heart of Our Message — 203

Conclusion — 213

What Others Are Saying About *Relentless*

Tom Rawls' passion for the local church and all that it can accomplish is inspiring. This is a good book for anyone who needs reminding of the beauty, power and true mission of God's Church.

CRAIG GROESCHEL
Senior Pastor of LifeChurch.tv
Author of *The Christian Atheist*

Tom's broad life experiences, coupled with his service to the Church have given him a unique perspective and understanding. This is a courageous and honest assessment of the Church in a biblical, historical and eternal context. I believe those who venture into these pages will see the Church from a more vibrant perspective – as profoundly powerful and vastly underestimated. These are strategic days in the history of the Church and we should do all we can to position her to fulfil her call and awaken the beauty within.

BRIAN HOUSTON
Senior Pastor, Hillsong Church

In all the years I've known Tom Rawls, I have always found him to be a strategic leader who challenges people's thinking to operate outside the boxes that restrict the Church from moving forward. This book will challenge, inspire and extend you.

DANNY GUGLIELMUCCI
Senior Minister, Edge Church International

I have known Tom and Denise for many years, probably too many! Tom has a big heart for the Church and this is reflected in his book *Relentless*. The title more aptly describes Tom! He is relentless in his pursuit of vision, and his passion for the Church is all pervading. *Relentless* is a timely book about THE Church, but also about A church. Pastors, leaders, volunteers and any student of the Church will enjoy the story of the Church, but especially one church on its journey of reshaping, change and ultimately growth. Challenging, witty, engaging and provoking – a must read for all.

DR SCOTT WILSON
Author of *The G Factor: Using Vision, Values, Goals and Strategy to Build a Church*
President of Eurolead.net.
Founder, Institute for Creativity, Leadership and Management (ICLM)

Tom Rawls has walked the leadership journey. Having spent years in a number of diverse cultures he is well equipped to write concerning the Church of the third millennium. Tom is well read, articulate and most of all passionate concerning the Church he sees shaping Europe's future. I found this book to be strongly prophetic, biblically balanced and instinctively futuristic and full of hope.

STEVE PENNY
Founder, On-Line Global Academy

It has been my joy not just to have known Tom Rawls for nearly 30 years, but to have had the privilege of spending wonderful times together (as young ministers) working on church planting projects and establishing our philosophy of ministry. Tom was always passionate and successful in the pioneering of a number of new churches across Australia, Asia and now the UK. He has consistently raised up strong leadership and has always sought the establishment of the body of Christ on real apostolic foundations. Tom has always been passionate about God building His Church and us having the blueprints. Much prayer and long periods of fasting laid his foundations strongly. He always seemed ahead in his thinking and constantly dared to push out into uncharted waters. This book is not theory, but a true challenge for the future, learned by a true church planter with strong, relentless, apostolic drive and passion. *Relentless* is a good description of my friend Tom Rawls!

TIM HALL
Evangelist and preachers.
www.timhallusa.com

Every since I first met Tom Rawls I have been impressed by his passion for God and his willingness to push the boundaries to see God's kingdom established on the earth. Two thousand years ago, Jesus said that He would build His Church, but what did He have in mind ... and does today's Church reflect His vision? In this book, Tom leads us on a journey, asking the tough questions and encouraging us to relentlessly pursue what Jesus really had in mind for His Church in our time. I highly recommend it!

MARK CONNER
Senior leader, CityLife Church, Melbourne, Australia
Author of *7 Strategic Changes Every Church Must Make*

In *Relentless* Tom Rawls gives us a compelling vision of the majestic force Christ's Church might become if she is willing to re-align herself with the revolutionary principles of the New Testament. He artfully and honestly combines his firsthand experience of re-firing the heart of an urban church with sound biblical ecclesiology. His call for leadership over management and spiritual potency over fatalistic defeatism, must not fall on deaf ears if the Western Church is to once more become Christ's "city on a hill".

MAL FLETCHER
Chairman 2020Plus,
Social commentator, author, broadcaster and futurist

Inspirational, energetic, charismatic, visionary, pioneering, and a man of faith. These are some of the things that come to mind when I think of Tom Rawls. I have known Tom for many years and he has always been an inspiration to me. I have seen him succeed in many areas of ministry. He has overcome difficulties and challenges and leads people into breakthrough and blessing wherever he goes. Tom is a man of outstanding ability and his book carries the spirit of faith that marks him as one of God's leaders of influence.

ALUN DAVIES
Senior Pastor of Faith! Church, Melbourne
Vice President of the Australian Christian Churches
President of ACC International

In John chapter one, the Bible says that the Word became flesh and dwelt amongst us. This is a book about just that – the Word infesting a man who has become relentless in his pursuit of changing the world for Christ. *Relentless* has always been the tattoo etched into the heart of Tom Rawls. In the 1980s he broke tradition and touched a youth culture for Jesus, in the 1990s he touched the world's underclass, and this century he is touching the Western world for Jesus. He has never relinquished, never quit, never backed down and never stopped. This book is infectious. You may become what you read.

DAVE GILPIN
Senior Pastor, Hope City Church, England
Author of *Sacred Cows Make the Best BBQ's*

RELENTLESS! What a great title for a book by my good friend and colleague, Tom Rawls. His objectives of inspiration, equipping and providing a road map for existing and new churches are clear and concise. Tom doesn't waste words or write from a distance. He shares from a genuine heart, his love for God, his love for Jesus Christ and his love for the Church.

Tom believes deeply and is committed to the fulfilling of all that God plans for His Church in Europe and the whole world. Tom's declaration, "I hear the sound of a generation rising with a roar, so full of energy that not even the armed forces of Hell will stand in their way," is very encouraging at a time when churches need to hear again from the Lord of the Church.

GEORGE FORBES
Former General Director of Assemblies of God World Missions
Leader of Mission Mobilisers International

I've had the privilege of knowing Tom Rawls for two decades, during which time he has been a pioneer of new paradigms and innovative church ministry. At the end of the first decade of the 21st Century, the Church is in transition. What we do now is crucial to the impact and influence of the Church in decades to come. This book is an important addition to the discussion of what the Church should be and how it needs to transform in order to fulfil God's purpose and lofty ideas for His Church. Tom's insights into the Church that is, and the Church that God wants to build, are inspiring and challenging.

ASHLEY EVANS
Founder, Influencers
Senior pastor, Paradise Community Church
National Executive member, ACC Australia
Co-founder, Family First political party

Relentless is a book of intense passion. Tom Rawls' and Christ's love for the Church on every page is highly contagious. This book is compelling reading and I highly recommend it to every church leader.

ASHLEY SCHMIERER
International President, Christian Outreach Centre
Author of *Fruit for Eternity*

Tom Rawls embodies everything that this book is about as he relentlessly pursues the dream of making God's Church great. It will stir your spirit and excite your soul to do the same.

LINDSAY AND JULIE CLARKE
President and Founder, Metamorphic International

Tom has done a brilliant job in communicating truth, wisdom and passion about the Church. Personal insight and experience is of huge benefit and value to anyone who needs a biblical understanding of who and what the Church is. I thoroughly recommend this book to *all* believers and leaders in the Church. What you don't know you can't communicate. This book will give you incredible knowledge!

JASON CASK
Senior leader, C7 Church, Glasgow

Tom Rawls LOVES the Church but HATES religion. His distinct humour and unique communication skill is refreshing and encouraging, yet it challenges us to grow and change. Tom lives out his love for Jesus and his belief in the local church, and his ministry is growing internationally because of his truly devoted life. I highly recommend *Relentless* and Tom's ministry in written form or in person. Tom is the real deal.

JACHIN MULLEN
Lead Pastor,
Word of Life Church, Red Deer, Canada

Tom Rawls is a wonderful preacher. He has the ability to deliver a message to hundreds of people with clarity and relevance. Yet, he can also connect you to that message in a way that makes you believe that it has been written just for you. He bridges the gap, breaks down the barriers and leads you straight into the arms of Jesus.

Tom is a leader yet he has the ability to "see" people. His passion is the Church, yet he knows the Church is made up of unique and valued individuals. His passion is healthy growth and development for those individuals and Christ's Church. Tom often says, "Can you hear my heart?" I am delighted to read this book and hear his heart through the words on these pages.

It is an honour to call Pastor Tom and his wife, Denise, my friends and to be part of our vibrant and healthy church that pro-actively reaches out to our city and beyond. My prayer is that this book is not only read worldwide, but that its readers will be impassioned and encouraged to step out in faith and build Christ's Church into the healthy, vibrant and beautiful entity Tom describes, the Church that God intended it to be.

MARIA LANDON
Author of the bestselling books *Daddy's Little Earner* and *Escaping Daddy*.

In this book my friend and mentor, Pastor Tom Rawls, will open your eyes to the radiant beauty that is the bride of Christ. Pastor Tom's heart and passion for the local church shines through each page, as does his realistic view of her. Thank you, Tom, for a fresh reminder of what we belong to.

JON COOK
Senior Pastor, Newcastle CLC

Pastor Tom Rawls is passionate about building strong, powerful churches and seeing the Church in Europe rise up to its full potential. This book is a clarion call to be involved in what Jesus is doing now. You will be challenged, inspired, motivated and moved. This is a must read for church leaders and everyone who wants to see change. In *Relentless* Tom calls us all to be the leaders and agents of change in Europe so that the Church of Jesus Christ can be all that it is destined to be. This book will inspire and stir us to action. I heartily recommend it.

JOHN GREENOW
Senior Pastor, Excel Church, Newton Aycliffe, UK

Whatever you do, don't be misinformed: *Relentless* is a great read! It is challenging, passionate and paints a majestic picture of the Church! Tom Rawls writes with a fresh and inspiring voice. It is clear in *Relentless* that he believes what Jesus said: "I will build MY Church!" Pastors and church leaders – get it, read it and pass it one to everyone in your church. I recommend this book.

MARK BATTERSON
Lead Pastor, National Community Church, Washington DC
Author of *Wild Goose Chase*, *In a Pit With a Lion on a Snowy Day* and *Primal*.

Tom Rawls crafts a verbal image of a Church that is expansive, passion-filled, relevant and accessible to the Google Generation. As you read this book a passion for the house of God will re-ignite and any excuses as to why "it's not happening" will be thrown out of the window as Tom's exuberance for what God is looking for in His Church in the 21st Century grips your imagination. Be inspired.

JAMES GALLOWAY
Senior Leader, Bethel City Church, Stoke-on-Trent, UK

Tom Rawls is a great man. When you spend time with Tom you are always inspired ... always! Tom is a great thinker and writer and as you read his journey in building the Church you find yourself not just reading words, but catching the passion of a courageous leader who is full of great insights. Tom, thank you so much for being you, showing us how to navigate in leadership and how to enjoy the journey.

BRENDAN WHITE
Lead Pastor, Hillsong Paris

Tom Rawls is a pioneer. He's a "journeyman" and he's been used by God to provoke thought and action. It has been an inspiration to watch him lead in his own unique style for almost three decades in three very different cultures (Australia, Thailand and the UK). All the while, he has retained a freshness in his approach to leadership, a passion to stay in touch with culture and a prophetic edge to his message. This book captures his quest for truth and relevance, his understanding of current trends, and his heart to see the Church be the unstoppable force its Founder meant it to be.

WAYNE ALCORN
National President of Australian Christian Churches,
Senior Pastor of City Church, Brisbane, Australia

I have known Tom for many years. In that time he has consistently been one of the most passionate church builders I know. Tom is relentless in His passion to see a thriving Church built in all corners of the world. He is also passionate about building lives that make up great local churches. This book will challenge you to view differently both the Church and your place in it. Read it if you are ready to be challenged!

NICK CAINE
Equip and Empower Ministries, Sydney, Australia

Dedication

I want to dedicate this book to the hundreds and thousands of courageous men and women who are planting local churches in difficult parts of the world. Many of these bold men and women will be persecuted and suffer for their faith. Some may even die for the cause of Christ as they labour to see local churches established that impact communities.

To quote my mentor and friend, George Forbes, I dedicate this book to "the church planters who are planting and leading local churches that are not 'mega-churches' nor are they ever likely to be," but are still touching their cities, communities and villages with the message of Jesus Christ. Many of these frontrunners of faith will remain nameless and faceless to us, but not to Christ. To Him who builds His Church they are champions of which "the world is not worthy" (Hebrews 11:38).

Acknowledgements

Very few could say that their book just "wrote itself." I feel the same. I want to acknowledge a few people who helped me write this book and get it published.

Thanks to my team of Owen Morgan, Phil Temple, David Kelly and Gemma Neill who read through the draft, making suggestions. Owen made many grammatical suggestions and I heeded almost all of them!

Thanks too to Laura Miles who painstakingly read every word, maybe three times, to correct more grammar, spelling, and help the flow of the book. You're awesome! Thanks to Lindsay Bruce for proof reading the text.

Thanks to Liz Morgan for producing the cover artwork for the book. I love it! You are incredibly creative.

I can't thank Tim Pettingale enough for his tireless work in editing the book. I'll never forget the first draft I sent to him and his gracious response! Since our first exchanges on email he has worked hard to make this book what it is. Thank you for your commitment to excellence on my behalf.

Thanks to my publisher, Jonathan Bugden, Director of Integrity Media Europe. I feel like he has become a good friend in the process. I love the way Jonathan wants each of his authors to feel like they are part of the family. Thank you for believing in me and the vision of this book.

Thanks too to my church, Proclaimers, in Norwich. What an awesome group of people who love me and support me as their pastor. I really love you. I am proud to be your pastor and to lead you. Thanks for following!

Finally, I want to thank my wife, Denise. Thank you for your support, your encouragement and your love for me. Thanks for releasing me for days and weeks to write when all I thought about was getting the next chapter finished. Thank you for being there. I love you.

Foreword

I first met Tom Rawls in the mid 1980s. He was leading a vibrant, groundbreaking church in Melbourne, Victoria. While Youth Alive was in its infancy, doing "live events" three or four times a year, Tom's church was having these kinds of services every week! One newspaper article perfectly summarised his efforts: "Rockin' Rawls has them in the aisles!" Tom was rocking the establishment way back then.

Our first meeting happened when Tom came to speak at the church where I served, long before Hillsong. He really impressed our senior pastor. Tom attended our Monday morning staff meeting and our pastor used him as an example of someone who was a "reader" and an "articulate speaker", telling us off and saying that we needed to be like that too. Some of us guys had an overwhelming desire to strangle Tom after that particular staff meeting. We took him out to lunch later that day and made him pay!

I next met Tom on a Thai Airways flight. I was about to take on the leadership of Hillsong London and Tom was on his way back to Asia. It was a chance meeting at 37,000 feet! Tom was trailblazing again, this time in another exotic location on the planet.

It was my privilege to next encounter Tom after he had assumed the leadership of Proclaimers, here in the UK. It was in the early days of his time in Norwich and I had the opportunity simply to be a friend during what he describes as, "a dark time in my ministry journey." Over lots of great coffee and a few great meals I was able to encourage him as he worked through a difficult transition to success. I told him back then that he would make it and it thrills me today to see him leading a cutting edge, 21st Century church in this part of the world.

Relentless, though not ground breaking in its information (after all, the data has been there for 2,000 years!) is a passionate, vibrant retelling of the Master Builder's desire, hopes and dreams for His Church, His Bride! Throughout, this book will inspire and challenge you as a leader and instruct you in the art of courageous leadership as you build with Jesus as a co-labourer of His great Church. This is a great book for people in any and every aspect of church leadership and is useful to provide anyone with a clear perspective on this awesome entity called the Church. Every church member should take the time to read it and imbibe the principles contained within.

I am continually humbled by what God is doing here at Hillsong London and amazed that anyone would use our story as an example of what God is doing in Europe today. But Tom has taken some of our story and used it to illustrate the good things God is fulfilling through but one branch of His Church. We are honoured and humbled, and we give all the glory to God as we champion the cause of the local church, along with Tom.

Let me say to those who are leading churches and feel overwhelmed by difficulties, politics and bureaucracy: *Relentless* will be a great source of comfort, inspiration and instruction. Those looking for a road map for what 21st Century Church could look like, THIS is the book! Get it, read it, study it and make sure every leader you work with has a copy as well. I recommend it to the broadest possible audience.

Tom is articulate and challenging in his approach. He brings a fresh voice and a new perspective as he unwraps well worn passages of Scripture. His passion for the Church is infectious. Before long you will discover that *Relentless* is not just about the Church, but about Tom's heart, which is a reflection of God's heart for His people.

Gary Clarke
Lead Pastor, Hillsong Church, London

Preface

The Church!

"Why did men worship in churches, locking themselves away in the dark, when the world lay beyond its doors in all its real glory?"
—Charles de Lint
(Celtic folk musician and story teller, b.1951)

"Christ and The Church: If he were to apply for a divorce on the grounds of cruelty, adultery and desertion, he would probably get one."
—Samuel Butler

"The blood of the martyrs is the seed of the Church."
—Tertullian
(Apologeticus, Chapter 50)

"And I tell you, you are Peter [Greek, Petros, a large piece of rock], and on this rock [Greek, petra, a huge rock like Gibraltar] I will build My church, and the gates of Hades (the powers of the infernal region) shall not overpower it [or be strong to its detriment or hold out against it]."
Matthew 16:18 (Amplified Bible)

I vividly remember the day of my daughter's wedding. It was my privilege to give her away that day. Before we left to go to the church there was just me and her in the house. Moments before we got in the car I told her that although she was being given to another man, I would always be her dad and would always love and cherish her as only a father can. She told me to stop because she was about to cry and it would make her mascara run!

I'll never forget how beautiful she was that day. We got in the car and I held her hand one last time as a single woman as we drove to the church. It was a thrilling day in every respect. The sky was blue, the sun shone brilliantly and there was a large crowd of onlookers, as well as our invited guests, to witness the day. Everyone was excited! My daughter was beautiful, dazzling in fact, as she prepared herself to walk into the church.

Just as every bride that walks down the aisle on her wedding day is beautiful, so the Bride of Christ is beautiful beyond description. Solomon, mirroring for us something of the great romance between Christ and His Church, tries to find words adequate to describe His passion for her beauty:

"How beautiful you are, my darling! Oh, how beautiful! Your eyes behind your veil are doves. Your hair is like a flock of goats descending from Mount Gilead. Your teeth are like a flock of sheep just shorn, coming up from the washing. Each has its twin; not one of them is alone. Your lips are like a scarlet ribbon; your mouth is lovely. Your temples behind your veil are like the halves of a pomegranate. Your neck is like the tower of David, built with elegance; on it hang a thousand shields, all of them shields of warriors. Your two breasts are like two fawns, like twin fawns of a gazelle that browse among the lilies."

It is an intimate, heartfelt, passionate expression of what Jesus feels for His people, His Bride, the Church.

This scripture seeks to portray an intimate, heartfelt, passionate expression of what Jesus feels for His people, His Bride, the Church. Yet words continue to fail us as we seek to understand Heaven's design for the Church He is building. Read on with a sense of reverence and awe ...

The Bride of Christ,[1] the House of God![2] This is the place of God's dwelling on earth; the body of Christ[3]. God says, "His eye is on it always and His heart is in it forever."[4] In the words of Jacob, "How awesome is this place!"[5]

The Church is the family of God in heaven and on earth[6]. The Church is the design of God born in the heart of God from eternity to become His plan on earth.[7]

She is prepared as a Bride for her Bridegroom, Jesus Christ, the Son of the Almighty God. She is beautiful and potent. She is diverse and divergent. She moves with a sense of harmony and accord. She has emerged through the centuries as a powerful, significant and influential force touching every corner of the globe.

Though she has experienced persecution, mistreatment and abuse, she continues through dangers, toils and snares[8] to be a light to the world[9] and a city on a hill.[10] Though she has experienced betrayal, treachery and has been downtrodden, she remains an indomitable light that refuses to be extinguished, to be quenched or to be obscured. She has known the infidelity of the times, yet remains rooted in the eternal strategy of God.

As the light of the world, the Church has lit the way for over 2,000 years and through the intense darkness of the ages she perseveres, relentlessly. Though some have displayed their disloyalty and unfaithfulness, her persistence has ever triumphed, defeating dictators, conquering kingdoms and piercing the shadows of jungles, deserts and rainforests the world over.

The Church is radiant and in Christ she is destined to be without spot or wrinkle, holy and blameless.[11] She is a glorious Church and her determination and resolve is relentless and resolute. She cannot be stopped, she cannot be silenced and she cannot be dismissed.

This Church has inspired countless men and women to extraordinary lengths. She has commanded the commitment of those who have gone on to change the world of their day. She has superintended the passions of many throughout the ages.

This awesome Church, moved by tenderness and grace, has

touched the broken lives of millions, influenced the course of history and brought healing to the troubled souls of the masses. She loves, she heals, she delivers and within her bosom she succours, brings relief and transforms those who embrace her and her Master.

This Church is not peripheral to the world.[12] She is unaffected by governments and galaxies, by politics or by the affairs of State. She is central to all of God's plans for the earth. Even her martyrs have encouraged her growth and influence.[13]

This Church is infused and steeped with a supernatural vigour, imbued with an energy so great, so fierce, as to have broken the very power of death and raised Jesus to new life.[14] This energy is so prevailing, so potent, that not even the schemes and plots of evil can thwart the forward movement of this triumphant Church. It is this same Spirit who invigorates and animates every aspect of the Church; the Spirit who raised Christ quickens every aspect of the Church.

She is a creative force in the world. She is original, remarkable and one of a kind. She is dazzling in her beauty, striking to behold and stunning as she moves through the ages. She is characterized by passion, she is fervour, she is ardour and she is zeal. She is stunning in her presentation and a genius in her speech. She is the Church of the living God.

The Church is a relentless and persistent force! There is ferocity and great strength. She is formidable, vigorous and has an overcoming spirit of Kingdom proportions. Not even the gates of hell can prevail against her.[15]

The Church is the most profound expression of Christ in all the earth. She is unrelenting, unyielding and unstoppable and she will never give up. She will never quit and she will never relinquish her mandate and her holy mission. She is the Church, the Bride of Christ, the Body of Christ in which He speaks and acts throughout the earth.

At the centre of this relentless Church is the majesty of our Lord Jesus Christ. Revelation 1:13-16 describes Him as, "Dressed in a robe reaching down to his feet and with a golden sash round his chest. His head and hair were white like wool, as white as snow, and his eyes were like blazing fire. His feet were like bronze glowing in a furnace, and his voice was like the sound of rushing waters. In his right hand he held seven stars, and out of his mouth came a sharp double-edged sword. His face was like the sun shining in all its brilliance."

Son of God and Son of Man, He who died and was raised from death leads this Church. He is the first and the last.[16] It is He who died but shall never die again! Jesus is the central character of this awesome Church and is the one who lives eternally. Proceeding out of His nature and character is an outstanding Church, potent beyond imagination, profound beyond comprehension.

As we consider this image of the Church from Scripture we marvel at her beauty, her glory and her relentless nature, but our breath is taken away when we behold Him who is the source of all her energy, creativity and wildness. Such majesty we behold! It is Jesus, the Alpha and Omega, the beginning and the end,[17] He is the source and wellspring of this supernatural energy and the Church is a grand reflection of His nature.

He is head to the Body, His Church.[18] He is the Great Shepherd to the flock,[19] His Church. He is the Lamb of God[20] who came to earth, clothed in flesh, to be the perfect and ultimate sacrifice for the sins of all mankind. He is Jesus and the Church basks in His reflective glory.

It is Christ Himself, the anchor of our souls,[21] who becomes the harbour of hope to those who are bereft of hope. He is wild, radical and fierce, yet He is the one who welcomes in the broken, the weak and downtrodden to fellowship with Him. He is the one who is moved to show forgiveness, grace and mercy to those who are in need.

This Church, whose head is Christ, greets a world in need of truth, life and vitality and He says to all, "Whoever calls upon the name of the Lord will be saved!"[22] [23]

Notes

1. Revelation 19:17
2. Hebrews 10:21
3. 1 Corinthians 12:27
4. 2 Chronicles 7:16
5. Genesis 28:17
6. Ephesians 3:15
7. 1 Peter 1:20
8. Lyrics of "Amazing Grace" John Newton, published 1779
9. Matthew 5:14
10. Matthew 5:14
11. Ephesians 5:27
12. Ephesians 1:22 Message
13. These words were recorded by Tertullian in his most famous work *Apologeticus* written in 197 AD
14. Romans 8:11
15. Matthew 18:16
16. Revelation 22:13
17. Revelation 22: 6
18. Ephesians 5:33
19. Hebrews 13:20
20. John 1:29
21. Hebrews 6:19
22. Romans 10: 13
23. The original inspiration for this section came from Robert Fergusson after listening to a message he preached in 2008.

Introduction

A dilemma

Leonardo da Vinci embodied the true spirit and essence of the Renaissance. He once said, "There are three classes of people: those who see, those who see when they are shown, and those who do not see."[24] Da Vinci was a visionary and a genius whose work I have studied for some time. A long time dream of mine had been to see for myself the most famous of all his paintings, the Mona Lisa, and that day came in January 2000.

During a trip to France Denise, my wife, decided to visit the Château de Versailles. Instead of going with her I went to the Louvre! It was snowing and a bitterly cold day, so I was thankful that the queue to gain entry was short. As I entered through the glass pyramid, went through the turnstile and proceeded down the escalator my heart was thumping with anticipation. I'd had this dream for over 25 years – one day I would see the Mona Lisa!

I almost ran to the place where the da Vinci was hanging.[25] Unbeknownst to me, I had passed two other of his paintings in my haste![26] But what did I care? I only had eyes for her! When I finally arrived at the desired spot, I stood a little distance away and just looked. I didn't want to ambush her.

Whilst standing there looking, imbibing the beauty, genius and sheer brilliance of the work, I phoned my mother. She was in Bangkok, home to us at the time, looking after our children whilst Denise and I were away. She asked where I was and I replied, teasingly, "I'm out with another woman." Knowing me well, she replied simply, "Okay!" Continuing undeterred I said, "Yes, she's very beautiful and possesses an enigmatic smile …" "Oh," she replied, "you're at the Louvre looking at the Mona Lisa." I was sprung!

I stayed there for a long time, I just couldn't get enough of this painting. I inspected it from various angles, getting a bit closer each time. Before I knew it, a whole hour had passed, but I hardly noticed, I found the experience so inspiring. I looked deeply into this woman's eyes, so expertly captured by the genius artist, contemplated the meaning of her subtle smile and just enjoyed the moment.

In the preface of this book my aim was to give you a similar glimpse into a work of art created by a divine Genius. In the same way that I was transfixed and inspired by da Vinci's painting, I pray that you will be sublimely inspired and challenged by the genius of God reflected in the incredible, organic entity that is His Church. I want to stir you to study afresh the Word of God and discover a fresh vision of all that we can become as the Church.

What I have written about the Church in the preface is absolutely true, but there remains a dilemma in the hearts of some. There will be many who, reading these statements of truth, will find them difficult, perhaps almost impossible to access. There is awesome strength and vitality within Scripture that describe "the Church", but nevertheless many will find it hard to grasp. As da Vinci said, some will see, some will see when they are shown, but there are those, sadly, who will not see. It is this latter group who will find the words of Jesus beyond their reach when He says in Matthew 16:18 (The Message) "I will put together my church, a church so expansive with energy that not even the gates of hell will be able to keep it out." But it is my sincere hope that, by the end of this book, that will change and those hard-to-reach truths will be accessible.

Many will look at the truths expressed in the Bible, make a comparison to the church they lead or attend, and ask, "Where is all this energy and power that Jesus speaks of?" Many will assert, to varying degrees, that their experience does not match up to what Jesus said they should experience. Others have lost faith in their church *ever* enjoying the weight and significance outlined in Scripture and, as a result, have given up hope and resigned themselves to going through the motions – adopting a "church as usual" mentality. Some leaders I meet fall into this category and are depressed and a bit embarrassed of their church's lack of power. Still others sneer openly at the grand claims of the Bible and wear their cynicism and disillusionment like a badge. Then, of course, there are those who are secretly broken-hearted, despairing and without hope – disappointed in God and His church, but they still soldier on.

Many will identify with these varying attitudes, so I ask, "What has happened to the Church in this new millennium?" Is it all over? Will the Church just eventually lie down and die? Are we all destined to irrelevance? What is happening to the Church?

Despite the negative views and bad press I believe something profound is taking place. There is a shifting, a realignment; there is a rumour going about. The winds of change and revolution are stirring once again. The dark ages of European church life are being peeled back, layer by layer, and influenced afresh with the same Spirit that raised Christ from the dead. All over the world, and in every language and culture, there is a quickening. The Church is arising again with power, influence and great momentum.

International leaders, like the sons of Issachar[27] of old who knew the signs of the times, have begun looking towards Europe as never before, laying foundations, spending time and money on leadership training, development and mentoring, as well as establishing new networks of pastors and leaders. There is a buzz, the message is getting around. Though only a whisper at this point in time, soon a great shout will go up: God is doing something in the earth once again!

As a Christian leader living in Europe I can certainly feel the winds of change. Things are moving up a gear and the mood is shifting from one of despondency and hopeless irrelevance to encouragement, a resurgence of powerful encounter with society and a vital connection with today. Things are being manoeuvred into position to create a power shift that will once again place Europe on the centre stage of the world. For too long the Church has been ignored; it is her time to rise again with vitality and energy.

As Malachi 4:2 says, "The sun of righteousness will dawn on those who honour my name, healing radiating from its wings. You will be bursting with energy, like colts frisky and frolicking."

Also consider the words of Habakkuk 1:5 which say, "Look at the nations and watch and be utterly amazed. For I am going to do something in your days that you would not believe, even if you were told."

We are living in prophetic times.

Defining terms

The title/subtitle of this book were carefully chosen, so allow me to explain why I wanted to capture that particular phrase:

Relentless describes the nature of the Church now arising here in Europe. Relentless can be defined as unyielding, adamant, steady and persistent.

The Church is unstoppable, inexorable, insistent and uncompromising. Something powerful, regal and ALIVE is rising from the ashes of a crumbling and apostate church mired in darkness, neglect and irrelevance. An awesome Church is being seen and heard and it is electrifying. This new brand of *relentless church* is rising with a spiritual aggression which stands in the face of every power of darkness, every principality and demonic stronghold and continues to take ground. She is arising with a face to the world which is filled with mercy, grace and justice for the poor.

The manifold wisdom of God is being made known through the Church.[28] The eternal purpose of God is being accomplished!

INTRODUCTION

The Church is on the threshold of significantly impacting Europe and the world even as we speak.

Renaissance is a word that was coined to describe the cultural movement which took place in Europe between the 14th and 17th centuries. The French word simply means "rebirth". It is an appropriate word to use because the Church is having its renaissance and it is happening right before our eyes.

500 years ago Europe was a hotbed of revival. Today Europe is one of the spiritually darkest places on earth, regarded by many as the greatest mission field on the planet. Europe, once home to such reformers as Luther, Calvin and Wycliffe, has become decadent and soulless. Europe has turned her back upon her great Christian heritage and has become apostate and backslidden.

But it is my conviction that Europe is poised to once again bring an injection of new life to the worldwide Church. Effective, passionate and intentional churches are rising up here, in some of the least likely places, and all over Europe I hear the sound of a generation rising with a roar, so full of energy that not even the armed forces of Hell will stand in their way. Even as European society looks on at the demises of leadership, strong, inspired leaders are emerging from these churches in Europe, leaders who sense not only the appointment of Christ but His empowering upon their lives. Churches of great impact are rising around Europe with a freshness that is grabbing people's attention and they have punch; they are beginning to move with verve and vitality.

These *renaissance* churches are sleek, stripped down, influential and vitally connected with today. Even though many are still small, compared to the world's mega-churches, they are gathering momentum and moving forward with a distinct and different flavour. They are pursuing excellence with a unique zest that impacts the world around them. Such "new breed" churches will pave the way towards renaissance thinking about the Church and how she engages with society; they will serve to impact the thinking and methodology of churches the world over. Watch and behold as they rise with influence and significance.

Theology: In an attempt to explain this part of the title, let me offer an explanation of the word "theology." Theology is the knowledge of God. Theology is vital because it helps us to understand God's nature and the Church that Jesus is building. Simply put, if we are ignorant of God's plan for His Church as laid out in Scripture, then we will not build local churches according to the original plan. Equally, if we don't truly believe what Scripture says about the corporate Church we will never see our local churches make the awesome impact they are intended to make. If we remain dull of hearing with stale hearts, ignoring the dynamic nature and character of God, we will fail to be a part of this outstanding building of living stones that Jesus so desires to see established in our world.

This book is not an exhaustive theology of the Church, but rather is intended to give a taste of excitement, the tip of the iceberg, something that hints of more to come. It employs a fresh and unusual style of exposition that I hope will get you thinking and reflecting upon Scripture. The expositions have a way of creating more questions than providing answers, but I trust they will cause you to dream and cause hope to rise.

This is no classic ecclesiology then,[29] but a fresh look at some well-worn scriptures that will inspire hope and a way forward for your church. I have faith that the Holy Spirit will inspire you and give you insight into what God desires for His Church on earth and in your city or community.

21st Century: With the 21st century as the backdrop of all we do it is vital we understand the changes, shifts and movements that are taking place before our very eyes. We live in a vital time of creativity, technology and of original thought. How the Church needs to keep its prophetic edge!

It is my opinion that the Church today reflects the early Church in its "pre-Christian" stance. Few people had heard of Jesus in the 1st Century, but the Church grew and impacted the culture and society of its day. Like the 1st Century Church we operate in a Christian vacuum where people know more about the life and times of the planet Pandora[30] than they do about Jesus, the Church or the Bible. Unlike the 1st Century Church, however, we are technologically advanced and have at our disposal all the 21st Century has to offer us. We must use that to which we have access to advance the message of Jesus and His salvation.

The aims of this book

I returned to church ministry and leading our present church after 12 years of missionary service in Asia. Instantly I became aware of how things had changed in the Church in just over a decade. Things were being done differently and I needed to get up to speed with God's programme. After a fertile period of learning it is my sense now that there is a need to articulate the theology of the Church for a new generation and communicate it with fresh hope and inspiration.

A renaissance theology for the Third Millennium Church is being written now by hundreds of brave leaders around the world and they need a platform for discussion. It has been a challenge to see this amazingly simple, beautiful and powerful Church rising afresh in the midst of the crushing darkness of today! It is my desire to articulate something of this awesome theology of the Church using some personal stories and fresh exposition of scriptures.

My goal for this book is twofold: firstly, to freshly inspire churches and church leaders worldwide to be all God wants them to be – that as we work with Jesus in this day we would be a light to the world. I want to put tools into the hands of leaders to help them build, as expert builders, a church that will be glorious like our Lord and Master Jesus.

Secondly, my goal is to provide, through sharing some of my own story, a road map to those wanting to "cross over" and breakthrough to establish the new breed of church God has ordained. I hope my stories and personal journey will infuse every church leader with optimism and faith.

I hope that this fresh look at the theology of the Church will help you to forge a powerful church built on the foundations of Jesus Christ, the apostles and prophets.

As you look with new eyes on these time-worn scriptures, allow your heart to be revitalised with love for God, His Church, and may He help you to build with confidence.

What's happening in the church needs to be shared with the world!

I hope this book encourages you.

Tom Rawls
October 2010

Notes

24. Leonardo da Vinci
25. The painting is situated in the Denon Wing of the Musée du Louvre in Paris, France
26. The other two paintings are, Portrait of a Woman and Saint John the Baptist
27. 1 Chronicles 12:31
28. Ephesians 3:10
29. Louis Berkhof's *Systematic Theology*, is one of my all time favourite theology books. Published by Eerdmans (September 1996)
30. From the movie *Avatar* directed by James Cameron

Part One

A RENAISSANCE OF LEADERSHIP

AND UNDERSTANDING

THE CENTRALITY

OF THE CHURCH

1

SOMETHING IS BROKEN

"I strongly believe that the responsibility of leadership is to shape the debate – to practice and project the right attributes – whether in a business enterprise, in our society, and even in our religions."
—Farooq Kathwari, CEO Ethan Allen

"You are the light of the world. A city on a hill cannot be hidden."
—Jesus Christ (Matthew 5:14)

"All of the great leaders have had one characteristic in common: it was the willingness to confront unequivocally the major anxiety of their people in their time. This, and not much else, is the essence of leadership."
— John Kenneth Galbraith

"Peter I have determined with gritty resolve to build my Church and it will be a powerful force – so expansive with energy that

even the designs of Hell will be unable to stop it. And guess
what Peter?
I will delight in using people just like you to make my dream
a reality!"
(A paraphrase of Jesus' words in Matthew 16:18)

Some of my story

I would say the last 50 years of my life have been pretty exciting! Others may disagree. I'm quite sure some have looked on with amazement and maybe a bit of confusion. I was born in America and moved to Australia at the age of 11, where I lived for about 23 years. After that my family and I moved to Asia and lived for 12 years in Thailand. Now we are living in the UK, so questions like "Where do you come from?" are a bit difficult for me to answer.

My ordination was a holy moment when, at 24 years of age, the leading figures of my denomination placed their hands on me and confirmed before a conference that I was called of God and separated for ministry. They used words like "ministry gift" to describe me at my ordination. Since that day I have seen the gracious hand of God placed upon my ventures and have experienced incredible fruitfulness over the years – a direct confirmation of His unique call on my life.

From 1979 until 1991 I was church planting in Australia. From 1991 until 2000 I was a missionary in Thailand, ministering throughout Asia with my denomination. The next three years were spent with World Vision, primarily in Bangladesh. Throughout this time I always sensed and believed in the call of God upon my life. So when my contract with World Vision was coming to an end and it appeared our time in Asia was concluding, I knew that God would lead us into something else – that He would use my 25 years of experience to impact and touch a city somewhere, maybe even a nation, maybe even the world? I believed I was about to embark upon the most significant thing I had ever done!

Norwich, England

I arrived in Norwich, England in July 2003. My return to pastoral ministry was a real challenge given the combination of "culture stress" and being back in the saddle of local church leadership after 12 years of serving as a missionary in Asia. I was an interesting combination of stressed-out Aussie and returning missionary "longing for the day," now living in the UK! Bangkok was a mega city of 12 million and Dhaka a city of 18 million, so waking up in rural Norwich, a city of only 350,000 people, was a culture shock. Still, I felt qualified for the role of pastor. I'd pastored churches before and I knew what I was called to do.

The leadership team I inherited in Norwich were businessmen with 10 years of experience functioning as "trustees"[31] of the church. The founding pastor, Bob Gordon, a man of great stature in England, had suddenly and unexpectedly died, leaving the church without any clear leadership succession. As is the case in such times, the burden of leadership fell upon the trustees to navigate the church through dark and trying times as they searched for a new leader.

Over the years this group of men had seen a lot and experienced some pretty ugly scenes while looking after the church. They had been forced to develop a particular paradigm of leadership I have since found is quite common in the UK, Europe, and many other parts of the world. But I believe there is a serious problem with this paradigm. Allow me to explain.

The problem of leadership

If you compare the inspiring view of the Church expressed in the preface of this book with the average European church, you will encounter a contradiction. As you read of the explosive growth of the early Church and look at the statistics of a dying Church in Europe, you will be faced with an inconsistency. As you look on at some of the mega-churches of the world or even those churches with great growth and impact in their cities, and then look at the church scene generally around the world, you will find yourself in a quandary. Something is not lining up!

Many modern day churches seem to have little or no connection with the powerful, impacting first century Church of the book of Acts. They seem to be two different entities. The book of Acts speaks of a powerful Church emerging from the day of Pentecost and 3,000 people being added to it in ONE day! It quickly grew to 5,000 men not including women.[32] The Jerusalem Church was a "mega-church" which some have estimated to be have 20,000 members[33] including women and children. It was a majestic thing to behold.

The message of the resurrection and salvation through Christ alone had gone throughout the world and it seemed nothing could stop the forward advance of the Church. Not only were Jews finding Jesus as their Messiah and being saved, but Gentiles were also coming to faith in Christ. From what could have become a backwater Jewish cult, Christianity exploded onto the world scene as an unstoppable movement. So relentless was the advance of the early Church that it reached every corner of the world before the end of the first century.

As we read the New Testament, we don't see an organisational structure outlined for the Church, though we do see some clear points of governance. The New Testament doesn't give us organisational diagrams or leadership flow charts, it teaches us some clear theology regarding the nature and character of the Church. One thing that is abundantly clear, however, is the need for gifted and spiritually empowered leadership in the Church. As the Lord added to the Church, He gave them gifts in the form of men and women supernaturally empowered to lead them. "Some were apostle, prophets, evangelists, pastors and teachers."[34]

These men and women were "ministry gifts"[35] otherwise known as ascension ministries, gift ministries or "Ephesians 4" ministries (from the scripture in which they are first mentioned). They included people like Peter, James and John, but there were others like Paul, Barnabas and Silas. The book of Acts makes an extensive list of these outstanding leaders and people of influence.[36]

Yet, the fact is, similar leaders in countless modern churches are having their gifting restricted by an unhelpful system of church governance.

Governance

Some of the greatest problems faced by the Church today are found in the area of governance. Churches are seeking to interface with and be accountable to governments and their own denominations. But, remarkably, we can see how secular governments and their values are adversely affecting the structure of local churches in an effort to make them accountable. Though the principles behind this desire are good and well-meaning, the form of governance imposed may not be.

Inadvertently, the Church finds itself trying to force its majestic structure of 2,000 years into a governmental and secular system that has been in place for merely 100's of years. We need a level of accountability to save our organisations and indeed our nations from the unscrupulous and unprincipled. But we, the Church, need to be faithful to New Testament principles without abrogating governmental values.

Look for a moment at the situation in the UK: legally, churches are considered charitable organisations and charities are typically run by a committee of trustees. In response to this legal requirement many churches in the UK and Europe have organised themselves as though they were in fact charities, i.e. like a club or a society, instead of a spiritual organism. These churches have mistakenly sought to structure themselves according to the legal framework laid down by the Charity Commission and Companies House.[37] But is this relevant for a body of believers?

Perhaps worse than this, Church denominations have imposed codes of governance on their own local churches, requiring the establishment of committees to exercise authority – despite the fact that according to the Bible, that authority should be reserved for those called as ministry gifts of Christ to the Church.

Such practices have had a material effect on the state of the Church. Many trustees of churches are more knowledgeable on the topic of charity law than they are New Testament Church principles. Some are following the rules and regulations of the Charity Commission over the biblical principles for governance laid down in the New Testament. Some board members know more about their denomination's constitution than New Testament principles of authority and leadership. By accident people have been turned into legalists, nit-pickers and unwitting denigrators of the Church of Jesus Christ. Tough words but true.

In England, as is the case in many places in the world, numerous churches have made their legal trustees the spiritual leaders of their church. Just one step removed from this scenario, there are churches whose board of elders or deacons, rather than being a repository of wisdom, insight and good advice, have become, by default, a committee of spiritual leadership who set the vision.

I believe it is fundamentally the rise of such committees, however they are formed and named, that has led the Church into decades of ineffective mission as they occupy a place that should be occupied by Ephesians 4 ministry gifts. It is a flawed model. God uses committees, but He does not lead His people through committees. Trustees, board members and deacons are valuable people, but should not be *leading* a church. Yes, they are part of a team of leaders, leading with others leaders, but should still be subject to a God-appointed, God-anointed leader. The fact that many are not is a problem to the future of the Church.

Such problems are further exacerbated when committee members exploit their positions and seek to usurp spiritual leadership by denigrating the role of appointed, anointed men and women, treating them as mere employees. When boards go beyond the boundaries of their remit, such actions are a transgression of the biblical pattern and scriptural principles.

I faced such a problem when I arrived in Norwich and soon discovered that it was far from unusual! When Bob Gordon died, the church's trustees reluctantly but firmly assumed the spiritual leadership of the church. I can understand why this happened. *Someone* needed to lead in the absence of visionary leadership and they did their best. In truth there was no one else to do the job.

But it is a big step to move from simply keeping the church/charity legal to assuming spiritual control of the church so as to keep its doors open for business. It is a role no board should undertake lightly and anyone finding themselves in such a position ought to ensure that, as quickly as possible, they place themselves back in a supporting role, working under an Ephesians 4 gift ministry.

In other parts of the world the picture, though different legally, is the same structurally. Churches tend to be governed and led by boards of elders or deacons. There is nothing wrong in having great teams of leaders, but senior leaders cannot be regarded simply as paid members of staff there to fulfil a job. Biblical principles are broken when someone other than an Ephesians 4 gift seeks to lead the church and dictate vision and direction. It's not necessarily a simple problem to rectify, I admit, but it is a real problem that needs to be confronted bravely by those who really care for the salvation of their cities.

Don't get me wrong.

I understand how this problem arises when major denominations across Europe and the world are struggling to get priests, vicars and pastors to sign on and, as a result, the spiritual leadership falls to those left behind.

I understand how this problem arises when there is a culture of pastors coming to a church for three to five years and then moving on to greener pastures.

I understand how this problem arises when pastors come and go, each with a different "God-given" vision. It's confusing! Someone needs to provide consistency and be there to clean up the mess.

But regardless of understanding the source of the difficulty, *it is still a problem!*

Other problems emerge

Combined with the problems of leadership and governance there is the endemic problem of the aging membership of the Church. Numbers are dwindling and attendance is falling off. Members of the Church are dying and their numbers are not being replaced. The Church is looking old. People are also leaving the Church, many of them young people. They echo Bono's words as they leave, "I still haven't found what I'm looking for."

Of those congregations who are hanging on, many are getting lost in a "time-warp", continuing to do church like they always have, inadvertently cutting off whole segments of society, specifically the younger generation. These churches have become mired in liturgy and stalled by traditions. There seems to be an inability to respond to societal trends. In many places the Church seems stuck, stumped and utterly mystified.

Perception conflicts

Our problems don't end here, however. The world looks on and thinks that church is boring. In the minds of many, the Church has become dull, tedious, nit-picking, hypocritical, judgemental, uninteresting, repetitive and our message and rituals meaningless! Just ask a few hundred people in your town, without prejudice, what they think. You'll be stunned. We are regarded by the general public as lost in our own world with no real answers to the plight of the human race and the deep needs of humanity.

Across many parts of the western world churches are closing down. Buildings are being made redundant and circuit preachers, looking after 4 to 6 congregations, are just conducting services in maintenance-mode, bereft of vision. They are merely providing a service to a group of people who will be dead in 20 years. Harsh some will say, but true. It was recorded in the newspapers that one major British denomination could close shop in 2040[38] with no one else coming to church and their buildings being converted to mosques. What a sad prediction!

To the world the Church often appears powerless and weak. It lacks the "wow factor". From the outside people look and say the Church is not moving in power. In many parts of Europe people regularly consult clairvoyants and spiritualists, and visit astrologists to have their tarot cards read. Practices of this nature are rampant worldwide while those who seek such spiritual guidance would never think of consulting a minister of the Church. Why? Because they perceive we have no power.

Ministers of the Church don't get off lightly either. They are frequently perceived as charlatans, critics or disconnected from the world around them. Many see church leaders as either hypocrites or puppets to the organisation. Others view them as either harsh and legalistic, or inept and lacking backbone. Many regard their sermons as sanctimonious and critical.

Something is broken

Over the years the influence of secular values on the Church has meant that the spirit of faith has been confined and restricted and God-appointed leadership has been subdued. As a result, not only does the world have a skewed picture of the Church, the Church is unsure of its own identity.

It's a big problem, but I know this: the Church cannot be run effectively by a committee of trustees, deacons' board or elders alone. Leadership is vital and a church cannot be led by a person who has no knowledge of the supernatural call of God and the gifts that accompany this calling. We can have good managers of churches, but the Church is desperate for real leaders who are anointed and empowered by Christ to bring vision, passion and growth.

Committees have their place and, if employed wisely, a lot can be achieved. But you can't lead a church with a committee – God-appointed leaders are vital! As Robert Copeland, the American author once said, "To get something done a committee should consist of no more than three people, two of whom are absent.[39]"

Some more of my story

When I arrived in Norwich it was with good references and twenty-five years of fruitful ministry behind me. I was not a novice. I had shared my views with the board before being appointed and made it clear that I believed strongly in a pastor/vision-led church leadership style. I explained what I understood a senior pastor was and how I believed one functioned in a New Testament church setting.

I knew the church was in transition, so from day one we were preparing for change. The most pressing need I could see was the transferral of responsibility for vision-setting and primary leadership from the trustees (as legal representatives) to me (as spiritual leader). Any scenario apart from that would detract from the effective running of the church.

Don't misunderstand me here, I wasn't trying to create a dictatorship where trustees and committees were no longer needed or valued. I simply understood from Scripture that the primary role of leadership and vision *had* to flow from the office of the senior pastor, so there had to be a shift of focus in the leadership.

I saw the role of the trustees in this process as one of facilitating this transferral of power, giving permission and moving back into their roles as legal guardians. It was essential that they make room for gifted leadership and allow the leader they had appointed to lead. I didn't expect this to happen immediately – I knew there would be a gradual process involved – but I saw in the first year of my leadership that they found this process very difficult and as a result, a great deal of conflict ensued.

The control which had been required for a number of years to keep the church alive, now needed to change. In its place anointed leadership and authority must be established if the church wanted to see future growth. To be blunt, the church had to be led by a God-appointed leader, not a group of businessmen, but these changes were difficult to navigate from all sides. Courage, along with great wisdom and insight was needed to walk this path. In fact, I walked with these men for over a year before making my appeal, but I was faced with opposition. The church had operated with a flawed model for many years and I sincerely believed that God wanted to usher in a new era of life and growth. Something was broken and it was being challenged. But my prescription did not go down well.

I've always been taught, and I see the principle clearly in scripture, that God's method is the right person in the right place and at the right time to put right the wrong. The first year was difficult, coming back to church ministry after 12 years was a challenge, but I worked hard and was a fast learner. The church grew from about 100 people to 170 in that first year. It was good, yet modest growth. During that time I was proving my leadership to the church and sought to work with those in existing levels of leadership, particularly the board. I could see that some fundamental changes were needed in the life of the church, apart from the method of governance, to make it truly effective. Some were really simple and others a bit more complicated. But navigating this proved to be difficult. A stronghold of thought and paradigm had developed and it was hindering the progress of the church.

I remember the night we faced the crux of the issues. I had organised a meeting with the trustees to discuss revamping the trust's deed, making it possible that I could also become a trustee and chairman – which to me was a natural part of assuming responsibility for leading the church. I had looked carefully at UK trust law and could see a way forward in the situation to bring change. I felt it was important for me as senior pastor to be a trustee and the chairman of the board to bring this legal entity back in line with biblical principles of leadership. Needless to say, the meeting didn't go to plan and some heated discussion ensued.

In short, my meeting was hijacked and it was made crystal clear to me that the trustees felt they had legal authority over me, since I wasn't a trustee, and that they defined my role simply as that of an employee. I was told they had absolute power and total authority regarding the running of the trust. As you can imagine, I didn't respond too well to this revelation. The committee was setting themselves up as the only ones with power and authority. As the pastor of the church I was expected to submit to them as a paid member of staff. They on the other hand felt no compulsion to be accountable towards me as their pastor. Here it was: we had a totally flawed model. What was playing out around me was not a reflection of New Testament leadership, but an attitude of control, an expression of the spiritual stronghold many throughout Europe are familiar with.

In their groundbreaking book *Sacred Cows Make the Best Hamburgers*[40] Kriegel and Brandt make this point: "People are the gatekeepers of change. They have the power to breathe life into a new programme or kill it." They continue by saying, "People's resistance to change is the most perplexing, annoying, distressing and confusing part of reengineering." Change is usually resisted unless a culture that embraces change is created. Control and power is a hard thing to give up for many. It's difficult to submit your opinions to someone else's when your opinions are the ones that have always mattered. It's not easy for your ideas to become just another point of view. Yet this is what those people who are not senior leaders in a church must learn to do. This flawed paradigm of governance is constraining the Church from becoming what God has called her to be. Men and women on committees stifling biblical leadership are keeping the Church weak and inept.

Alongside the good and well-meaning people occupying positions on boards are people who have become prickly people in power. They themselves are not ministry gifts of Christ according to Ephesians 4:11, yet they want to lead the church as if they were. Some have become control freaks and lovers of their power. Some actually believe that if they were to pull their financial "support" the church would just crumble. This attitude of control is a dark and malignant spirit that takes a church away from its biblical roots and turns it into something the Master Designer never intended it to be. In these cases there are power plays, any issue becomes "political", and it is amazing to watch the transformation of the church into something other than the House of God.

I have discovered hundreds of churches in this position where trustees, boards, elders, or deacons, whatever you call them, rule and lead the church. These committee people have seen pastors come and pastors go and control becomes a battle royal. Some pastors and leaders are literally powerless to bring change and so have resigned, leaving the church once again in the hands of the unqualified and those not called. Others leaders are forced out of their churches by powerful personalities on the committee, while others just hang in there to live a comprised and disheartened existence for a few more years, heartbroken and without vision

One pastor I know in Europe just resigned because he realised it would be too costly a thing to move forward. His need for courageous leadership never eventuated so, bless him, he quit. I know of one pastor forced to step down by his board because he wasn't doing things to their liking. How sad it is when churches are led by personal preferences rather than biblical principles. (Let me pause to say this: I do not condone the activities of brutal leaders who pay no respect to others and seek to walk all over people. This is a true violation of the ministry God has given to us as leaders.[41]

I have worked with a number of fine men and women of God who are seeking to break this pattern and stronghold over church life. They are heroic people who are rising up to be all they were called to be in God. But while I have heard of successful "crossing over" experiences,[42] I have heard many heartbreaking stories where sincere, godly pastors have been trampled and broken. I watch with delight as young men and women go out to launch new church with a fresh paradigm of New Testament leadership, and I watch with sadness as churches which are decades old struggle to find new life and relevance in our 21st century.

The need remains for a fresh understanding of what the Bible says regarding leadership and governance. I am astounded that Christian leaders are so ignorant of what the Scriptures teach regarding the Church. Some organisations would prefer to listen to the rhetoric and rituals of their denominations than to what the word of God says about the Church. One denominational leader I spoke to said, "I'm in charge here. The last thing I need is an overzealous pastor running around with his Bible in hand claiming he is a gift of Christ to the Church!"

My experience with pastors and leaders has confirmed to me that the attitude of some of these trustees, elder, deacons and boards is sincere, godly and truly servant-minded, but many of them just don't get it. As da Vince said: "There are those who don't see." Some of these committee people don't understand the concept and flow of New Testament leadership. They confuse

God's will with their personal desires and are ignorant of New Testament theology concerning the Church, its mission, its motivation and its leadership responsibilities. As a result, many of God's leaders live well below the expectations of biblical leadership.

Something needs to change! Consider the words of Jesus in Mark 2:21-22: "No-one sews a patch of unshrunk cloth on an old garment. If he does, the new piece will pull away from the old, making the tear worse. And no-one pours new wine into old wineskins. If he does, the wine will burst the skins, and both the wine and the wineskins will be ruined. No, he pours new wine into new wineskins."

Notes

31. In the UK the term "trustee" is used to describe the legal representatives of the church before the Government and specifically the Charity Commission. In other contexts this term could be used to describe the elders or the deacon's board or just the committee who assist the leader in leading.
32. Acts 4:4
33. 5,000 men – add to that women and children
34. Ephesians 4:11
35. This is a word I will use repeatedly through the text of this book; I am talking about those who are gifts of Christ to the Church as per Ephesians 4:11.
36. Romans 16:7 speaks of Andronicus and Junias – it appears from the text Junias was not only an apostle, but a female! Acts 14: 14 refers to Barnabas as an apostle; Acts 15: 40 refers to Silas as an apostle; 1 Thessalonians 1:1 and 2: 6 speak of Timothy as an apostle; Paul refers to Apollos as an apostle in 1 Corinthians 4:9, 4:6 and 3:22; James the Lord's brother is mentioned as an apostle in Galatians 1:19.
37. This applies specifically for the UK.
38. Telegraph article written by Jonathan Petre, Religion Correspondent, Published 3rd September, 2005
39. Thinkexist.com
40. Robert Kriegel and David Brandt , *Sacred Cows Make the Best Hamburgers*. Published by Harper Business in 1996
41. See Jeremiah 23:1-2.
42. Paul Scanlon, *Crossing Over*. Sovereign World, April 2003

2

FIXING THE PROBLEM

"Control is not leadership; management is not leadership; leadership is leadership. If you seek to lead, invest at least 50% of your time in leading yourself—your own purpose, ethics, principles, motivation, conduct. Invest at least 20% leading those with authority over you and 15% leading your peers."
— Dee Hock
Founder and CEO Emeritus, Visa

"You can structure for control or you can structure for growth, but you can't structure for both."
—Nelson Searcy
Pastor of the Journey Church Manhattan

"Dictators ride to and fro upon tigers which they dare not dismount. And the tigers are getting hungry."
—Winston Churchill

> "Like a will that takes effect when someone dies, the new covenant was put into action at Jesus' death. His death marked the transition from the old plan to the new one, cancelling the old obligations and accompanying sins, and summoning the heirs to receive the eternal inheritance that was promised them. He brought together God and his people in this new way."
> (Hebrews 9:16, The Message)

In the midst of this leadership malaise in the Church I see encouraging signs of a new Church rising and it gives me great confidence. The most profound aspect of this new breed of church is that they are led by outstanding people gifted by Christ. The Church needs such God-anointed individuals, leaders who are courageous, skilful, called of God, and empowered by the Holy Spirit. The Church is desperate for leaders to become all they can become in God.

It remains my opinion that when God sees a problem He sends *someone* to fix it. No amount of money will fix the problem; it won't be a new programme, a new leadership structure or a new event. God sends *people*. Someone once said, "Leadership is the problem and leadership is the answer." I agree.

Who should lead?

Harry Truman once said, "Men make history and not the other way around. In periods where there is no leadership, society stands still. Progress occurs when courageous, skilful leaders seize the opportunity to change things for the better."[43]

As Jesus builds His Church He takes great delight in using people to co-labour and co-lead. Once the right person is in place and leading, God can speak and move through that person. The Bible teaches that having the right person at the helm of leadership will open the door to success.[44]

I love the passage of scripture in Joshua 1:5–6 that says, "No-one will be able to stand up against you all the days of your life. As I was with Moses, so I will be with you; I will never leave you nor forsake you. Be strong and courageous, because you will lead these people to inherit the land I swore to their forefathers to give them." It affirms how God backs his chosen leaders.

God was with Joshua and as long as Joshua stood with God no one would be able to stand against him. God promised to "be with" Joshua and never leave him or forsake him, that if Joshua would be strong and courageous he would lead the people to inherit the land! This passage encourages us to stand and be courageous leaders with the sense that God is with us. This is not a licence to become a little dictator or an authoritarian leader, but to recognise the hand of God upon our lives and lead with integrity whilst developing those around us.

God does not lead His church through committees. Anything with more than one head is a monster! God's principle of effective leadership is placing His hands upon a person, anointing them, calling them, equipping them and speaking to them. In a signature portion of scripture Paul expands on this thought:

> "And he gave some, apostles; and some, prophets; and some, evangelists; and some, pastors and teachers; for the perfecting of the saints, for the work of the ministry, for the edifying of the body of Christ." (Ephesians 4:11-12 KJV)

Jesus gave these ministry gifts to the church. In a verse prior to verses 11-12, in Ephesians 4:8, we read that Jesus, "… gave gifts to men." The word "gift" here is different from the word used for the gifts of the Spirit (charismata) meaning a divine endowment. The word employed here in Ephesians 4:8 is the Greek word *doma*.

The concept embodied in the word "doma" is that Christ, when He ascended on high, gave gifts of men and women (apostle, prophets, evangelists, pastors and teachers) to the Church. In simple terms Christ, in the process of building of His Church, has designated particular men and women as leaders of His church; they are Christ's gift to His body. These individuals don't just have a gift, they *are* the gift. These distinctive people are distinguished not because of gifting they possess, but because they are themselves the gift. They have a call upon their lives that is recognised by others who are also called. These individuals are separated and endowed with abilities from the ascended Christ. They have been specially prepared by God.[45] They are gifts to the Church and to be valued and honoured.

I find it interesting in Scripture how these ascension ministry gifts are recognised. One example is found in Acts 13:1-3 where Paul and Barnabas are "set apart" or recognised as ministry gifts of Christ. "In the church at Antioch there were prophets and teachers: Barnabas, Simeon called Niger, Lucius of Cyrene, Manaen (who had been brought up with Herod the tetrarch) and Saul. While they were worshipping the Lord and fasting, the Holy Spirit said, 'Set apart for me Barnabas and Saul for the work to which I have called them.' So after they had fasted and prayed, they placed their hands on them and sent them off."

Notice prayer and fasting here, along with the laying on of hands. However it's done, I don't want to be too prescriptive, we see here two men being recognised as ministry gifts, both called as apostles, and set apart for that work.

To assume the role of an Ephesians 4 gift ministry needs the recognition of others. Some people look at their minister's credentials and say, "It's just a piece of paper." But it is so much more than that. What that piece of paper says is that this person has been recognised, approved by a body of other leaders and deemed to be called and appointed by Jesus Christ to serve as a leader in His Church.

Practically speaking the book of Revelation gives a glimpse of this principle. John is asked by Jesus to transcribe letters to the seven churches. Notice to whom they were addressed, "To the angel of the church write ..."[46]

The word angel is, according to Strong's Concordance, aggelos[47] (ang'-el-os); from aggello, a messenger; especially an "angel"; by implication, a pastor.

The Living Bible, I believe, rightly paraphrases this verse by translating Revelation 2:1, "Write a letter to the *leader* of the church at Ephesus and tell him this."

Now, we know leaders don't lead alone and neither should they be a law unto themselves. They are not to be dictators or lead in an authoritarian style. But when Jesus desired to speak to the churches of Revelation He wanted to address the "messenger" or leader.

Revelation 1:20 goes on to help us in our understanding:

> "The mystery of the *seven stars that you saw in my right hand* and of the seven golden lamp stands is this: *The seven stars are the angels of the seven churches*, and the seven lamp stands are the seven churches."

In other words, the "angels" or leaders of the churches are like stars in the hands of Christ. We seem happy to accept that the Church is like a lamp stand, a light to the world, a city on a hill, but we baulk when we see in the same passage that the leaders of the Church are like stars! Thankfully, they find themselves in the very hands of Christ. The hand of Christ provides both protection and guidance to these gifts to the Church and will be swift to also bring discipline and correction when needed.

The new Apostles ...

Throughout Scripture we see this principle of God sending someone to fix a problem in operation. It's not a new thought.

> Noah built a boat that saved his family
> Abraham was the father of faith

> Moses went to talk with God in the wilderness and became the leader of the Jewish nation, leading them to their promised land
> Joshua was the one who led the armies into battle
> Caleb led his family to take the mountain he was promised
> Had it not been for Joseph the people of God would have starved and vanished from the Earth
> The Jews were ruled over first by judges. Note the principle: Judges 3:9 says, "But when they cried out to the Lord, he raised up for them a deliverer, Othniel son of Kenaz, Caleb's younger brother, who saved them."

When God wants to do something new in the land He raises up a deliverer, a leader. Old and New Testament examples are prolific. With the 21st Century as our backdrop, however, many of the people Jesus is sending to the Church look a little different to their biblical counterparts. Some of the apostles, prophets, evangelists and pastor-teachers who serve growing churches work in media, graphics and finances; they possess web and communications skills. They have been prepared in their secular jobs to lead and work effectively in God's Church.

These specially gifted people may not have gone through a Bible College or Seminary but were medical doctors, occupational therapist or managers in the finance departments of large companies before their giftedness to the body was recognised by other leaders. There is no doubt though, that they are called by Jesus to lead. They have been sent by Jesus as His gifts to the Church, to function within His body as specially gifted people. They don't look like John the Baptist, wearing camel skins and eating grasshoppers, but we see them rising within the body, people heaven-sent to fulfil destiny and achieve greatness.

Not all of these gifted people will be mandated to lead as senior leaders, but will go to make up an influential team of gift ministries. Notice that during missionary journeys Paul always took others with him who were also apostles, like Barnabas and Silas. There was no doubt that Paul was the leader, but he was accompanied by other gifted ministries who complemented the team.

Modern churches need similar gift-mixed teams. Senior leaders of growing churches need to surrounded themselves with people gifted by Christ. Such teams are essential to the effective running of the church. Such teams move with a sense of destiny, but work together with a sense of consultation and consensus. But no one would ever mistake who actually leads this team of gift people. In every team like this there is always a senior leader.

The call

Scripture demonstrates extensively the concept of divine calling. Take the story of Isaiah. God asks, "Whom shall I send?" and Isaiah, dazzled by the awesome vision of His throne room and flying angels simply says, "Here am I. Send me!" (Isaiah 6:8). The concept of being "sent" is powerful.

Look at how Paul introduces himself to the Church: "Paul, a servant of Christ Jesus, called to be an apostle and set apart for the gospel of God" (Romans 1:1). He was "called" and he answered the call. Paul was a great scholar of his day – a man lauded for his academic achievements – but through a series of unique events he answered the call to be an apostle. I love the fact that he refers to himself as a servant of Christ first and an apostle second. It forever puts into context what our leadership should look like: servant hearted and servant minded; never dictatorial or despotic.

Jesus answered His call too.[48] God sent Him into the world[49] to provide the way of salvation. God put on flesh and moved into the neighbourhood. The perfect Son of God came into a very imperfect world to give Himself as a perfect offering for the sins of all mankind. He was sent by God to deal with the most powerful of enemies, sin and death, and He won a great victory. This victory was accomplished on our behalf and salvation came to the world. We understand the power of Jesus being sent into the world, we now need to understand the impact of being sent by Christ into the world.

The role

What was to be the role of these sent men and women? How were they to function? What were the parameters set for them? Paul, in vivid colour, explains. Ephesians 3:8-11 is a powerful reminder to us all of the intent of God.

"Although I am less than the least of all God's people, this grace was given me: to preach to the Gentiles the unsearchable riches of Christ, and to make plain to everyone the administration of this mystery, which for ages past was kept hidden in God, who created all things. His intent was that now, through the church, the manifold wisdom of God should be made known to the rulers and authorities in the heavenly realms, according to his eternal purpose which he accomplished in Christ Jesus our Lord."

Paul declares that the intentions of God are clear and unambiguous. *God's intent is that through the agency of the Church* His wisdom will be made known to the world around us. Into the hands of the Church, led by His appointed people, a great commission has been given. It is the Church that will superintend God's eternal plans for the world and do so according to the eternal purpose accomplished in Christ Jesus our Lord. Notice here that buildings don't superintend this mystery, only people can do it!

Notice also the word "purpose". It is singular, not plural. God doesn't have "purposes" He has a purpose. This purpose is what has driven and motivated the Church for the last 2,000 years. It is through the Church that God intends to make known the glory of His plan of redemption and salvation. The greatest challenge for the Church now is to transition from what it has become to what it could become.

I am torn as I look across Europe. I have a saying, "It is easier to give birth than to raise from the dead." In other words, it may well be easier for new churches to be planted than for old churches to transition. As true as this is it is not impossible for an old church to learn new tricks. It takes a process, it takes a commitment to change, it requires a clear understanding of New Testament leadership principles, and it takes courage, faith and a willingness to risk. Above all it requires a relentless sense of intentionality. I believe this book will help churches who are willing to do the hard yards and make the transition.

The power source for ministry

In laying the foundations for His disciples' future ministry, Jesus was very careful to give strict directions to them before He ascended into heaven.

The first instruction was to wait for the Holy Spirit. Luke 24:49 says, "I am going to send you what my Father has promised; but stay in the city until you have been clothed with power from on high."

Acts 1:5, 8 says, "For John baptised with water, but in a few days you will be baptised with the Holy Spirit. But you will receive power when the Holy Spirit comes on you."

Jesus wanted to ensure that the first leaders of His Church were full of power and fire from Heaven. He wanted to emphasise to each of them how essential it was to be supernaturally equipped to do the job. This word of instruction was not just to leaders but the whole body of Christ.

Following on from Jesus' instructions, Paul teaches that there are men and women who have received grace for ministry. "But to each one of us grace has been given as Christ apportioned it.

This is why it says: "When he ascended on high, he led captives in his train and gave gifts to men" (Ephesians 4:7-11).

Paul teaches that there are some amongst us who have *received grace* to operate as apostles, prophets, evangelists, pastors and teachers. This grace has not been given to every believer, but a special group of men and women who have received grace have been called, appointed, and equipped to lead the Church. They are infused with power, supernatural skills and godly talent. The problem in many churches is that there are men who are not graced with these leadership gifts seeking to lead as if they are – be they part of a committee, a board or a team of deacons. Conversely, we have the problem that many men and women who are graced to lead are fearful to do so because they don't want to upset their board. Or, they are so overwhelmed with maintaining the programme of the church that they are too busy to lead effectively. There are also men and women in positions of leadership who have succumbed to the temptation of just going through the motions and have no real relationship with God. They become fire fighters instead of fire starters.

But here's where things are really broken: there are leaders who don't really believe the Church is the hope of the world. There are leaders who have given up on the Scriptures, who no longer long for spiritual power and grace and have become fearful of stepping up to communicate the message of God. They are blinded to the great majesty and potential of the church they are supposed to be leading.

More of my story

When I arrived in Norwich I came with a word from God and I believed I was in the city, "for such a time as this". When I was asked to become the leader of the church in Norwich it was because the church needed a spiritual leader or, I was told, the church would fold and be shut down within six months.

About twelve months into the journey I was having a disagreement with the trustees and I paused in our discussion and said, "Guys, you called me. Come on now, if you could have done this without me you would have, but you couldn't do it. This is why I am here. I am the leader of this church. *I am here, now please let me lead.*"

It is tragic when the visionary leadership of a church is allowed to fall into the hands of those who are not mandated as gift ministries. It is even more tragic, when a real leader is present, that a committee should struggle to hold onto its power instead of graciously moving sideways and making room for God's leaders to lead. In such a situation all kinds of unbiblical actions take place. Wrong attitudes are allowed to remain, bad behaviour runs rampant and division is brought into the body of Christ. In the end it's the church that suffers and people get hurt.

I know being a trustee (replace that with elder, deacon, board member, church leader or department leader) can be a thankless job. No doubt there are those who have had to hold together a weak and failing church and have experienced hurt and pain as a result. I have no wish to undermine good people placed into tough situations. Some of these same people will have struggled for years with a man or woman who was not a God-anointed gift ministry.

I am reminded of a situation just like this where the senior minister of a church in Europe is fighting with his elders. He says they are overbearing and stuck in a rut. The truth is he has shown traits of laziness and is not being effective in his leadership because he refuses to grow and develop in exercising the ministry God has given him. It is heartbreaking to see these kinds of leaders not leading at the level Christ has called them to lead.

However, I pause to speak from a clean and open heart towards God. My experience in church life for over thirty years now has led me to believe that some of these board members or trustees have, over time, become carnal, worldly, seditious, political and at times just downright mean. They think they are right and push an agenda not born in the heart of God which brings division, heartache and trouble to the church.

I once heard a pastor speak about a deacon possessed church! I heard another pastor say he had no desire to go to Heaven when he heard there were four and twenty elders there![50] I remember hearing another story where one church board member, who wanted a certain leader in the church to be dismissed, approached the senior Pastor with the words, "I think I have given enough money to the church over this last year to get my wish." The senior pastor, with a number of other church leaders, went to this man's home that night with a cheque for the amount of money he had given the church that year. They confronted him with his bad behaviour, presenting him with the cheque. His response was to joke and make light of it withdrawing his request and tearing up the cheque. This is gutsy leadership at its best! I love it.

Exerting spiritual force

Hindsight is awesome! There is no doubt as I look back on my journey that I could have been a bit more gracious in dealing with certain people and situations. I could have been more prayerful and sensitive, been less aggressive and shown more wisdom. But there are times, like the story above, when a leader needs to exert spiritual force.

Leadership is not dictatorship. Wise church leaders understand the need for others around them to help them lead. They want people to "buy in" and have a sense of ownership in the church. Great leaders spend time garnering this kind of consensus and building effective teams. But in a conflict situation we need to remember that God will fight for His leader if that leader has committed themselves to walking in integrity. It is never a wise thing to fight against God appointed leaders.

Hebrews 13:17 brings clear and somewhat provocative instruction: "Obey your leaders and submit to their authority. They keep watch over you as men who must give an account. Obey them so that their work will be a joy, not a burden, for that would be of no advantage to you."

The word "obey" – *peitho*[51] – means to agree with, confirm, believe in, have confidence in, obey, trust in and yield to. It means a lot more than just blindly doing what you're told. It doesn't give a leader the right to order people about, quoting this scripture and using it like a cricket bat, smacking people over the head who don't get it. Those being led by this person should confirm their leadership by flowing with them not against them. They are called upon by Scripture to believe in their leaders, have confidence in them and trust they are hearing from God. Wise leader have forums to garner consensus and to consult others as they direct the affairs[52] of the church. Their aim is to get agreement and see others walking in harmony.

The word "submit" – hipeiko[53] – means to yield or to be "weak". It means to surrender your point of view or your opinion to leadership. Again, this is not an opportunity for a leader to bend people to their will by forcing them to do things they don't want to do. Submission is an act which men and women are inspired to perform in the presence of wise leaders who cast vision and exercise God-given giftings. Wise leaders give people time and space to yield and defer to them and should take care not to force issues. Voltaire once said, "Opinion has caused more trouble on this little earth than plagues or earthquakes."[54]

I heard it this way, "Opinions are like belly buttons. Everyone has one and they're all full of fluff!" There comes a time in every dynamic leadership situation where people are called to simply surrender their opinions, personal preferences and positions and flow with their leader. Again I say, this is not an opportunity for a leader to bully to get his or her way, but to work patiently with others[55].

Working together in teams is essential. In every scenario of church leadership you need men and women to come alongside to assist you in the work of the Lord. I believe in leadership teams, but I also believe Scripture supports the concept of "first amongst equals."

In my situation I had been called to lead, I was anointed and appointed by God and I had even been legally "contracted" by the board to lead, but the way forward was consistently blocked by these same men who simply did not understand their role had changed. Even though I pleaded with them for reconciliation it appeared the cause was lost. It's sad when people disagree and they divide and separate, yet it gives God the opportunity to approve one over the other.[56]

As a pastor I had a vision from God: I wanted to see the church grow into a large and significant church that could "take the city" for Christ. I believed I was the man to bring this church into impact, influence and effectiveness. I believed I was about to walk into the most significant thing in my life. I had an overriding sense of destiny! It was in my DNA to build a church culture that was motivated by Christ's cause to seek and save those who were lost. I wanted to work in cooperation with the Holy Spirit to build a generous kingdom culture. It was in my heart to see a church moved by a desire to serve, to pursue excellence in every area.

Strangely these men, who were the committee, also believed this about me. Right up to the end of our differences they stated that I was God's man for the job. Equally strange was their reluctance and stubbornness to the end to actually let me do that job and graciously move with me.

These kinds of churches don't just happen, there is a process and a need for consistent and exacting intentionality on behalf of its leaders. The church has to be brought under the control of the Holy Spirit and placed in the hands of a ministry gift of Christ. It requires the kind of courageous, visionary leadership that makes some people very nervous! The process of transition we're talking about doesn't just happen either. Spiritual force is needed. In my situation there were a number of clear and identifiable strongholds that needed to be dislodged.

Fasting prayer

Inadvertently, a spiritual dynamic was put into action in our church when, in April 2004, we embarked on a 40-day fast. It was awesome as folks all over the church began to pray and fast for a breakthrough, and we got one – just not the way I had wanted it to be. Most of the spiritual power needed to transition and bring change to the church came from the fact that as a church we sought God in fasting prayer. Imagine the amount of energy building as over 100 people sought God for a breakthrough for more than six weeks!

I won't give you the blow by blow saga that followed and continued through June to December of that year. It was ugly and unpleasant. Suffice to say it was a tough time for everyone involved. Personally, I wept, was sleepless for many nights and questioned my sanity. There was always going to be a cost for such a church, but I didn't think it would hurt this much! But breakthrough finally came in December 2004 when we moved from our old premises, a building owned and controlled by a former member of the church with aspirations for leadership, and we moved to a hotel conference centre literally just two miles down the road. Difficult it may have been, but it was our defining moment, our finest hour, we were moving out. The old trustees didn't want to move with us and so they moved to other churches within the city. Sadly, their decisions removed them from relationship with me and ultimately removed them from fellowship with the church. Their actions in turn caused division in the church. In our move to the hotel conference room we lost around 80 people in the process. This was incredibly painful to me and Denise, but how much more painful is it for the heart of God when men decide not to stand together in unity?[57]

This book was born in my heart

Through tears, many hours of depression and through much self-doubt I believed that one day I would write a book that would hopefully inspire other leaders to "pay the price" for courageous leadership and walk the road to significance.

As I walked up and down my front lounge room in the early hours of the morning praying, unable to sleep because of worry, I trusted that it would all pay off one day; this would not be a wasted experience. It was a trial I would go through to encourage and inspire others to do the same! And in the process I believed God would grant me the privilege of pastoring an awesome new breed of church in the UK that would influence many others in Europe to be effective, significant and truly 21st Century. I believed that God was calling me to become a "cultural architect" for His kingdom, to lead an audacious group of people into an adventure of building a new kind of church. This culture would truly be a kingdom culture that would have a massive impact. I prayed that our church would become a relentless and unstoppable force imbued with the Holy Spirit's power; a bold church ready to touch the city and beyond; a church with clear vision and a potent set of values that were biblical and infused with God's power.

The motto of our new church was to become a place that would "reach people, influence culture and build future." This is what we are becoming today.

Notes

43. Thinkexist.com
44. 1 Corinthians 3:3–9
45. Jeremiah 1:5
46. Revelation 2:1
47. NT32 Strong's Reference
48. Matthew 10:40
49. John 12: 49
50. Revelation 4:4
51. Strong's Concordance NT3982
52. 1 Timothy 5: 17
53. Strong's Concordance NT5226
54. Thinkexist.com
55. 2 Timothy 4: 2
56. 1 Corinthians 11:19
57. Psalm 133

3

BECOMING AN EXPERT BUILDER

"The loftier the *building*, the deeper must the *foundation* be laid."
—Thomas Kempis

"For he was looking forward to the city with foundations, whose architect and builder is God."
(Hebrews 11:10)

"We turn to God for help when our *foundations* are shaking, only to learn that it is God who is shaking them."
—Charles C. West

"He who walks with the wise grows wise, but a companion of fools suffers harm."
(Proverbs 13:20)

Wisdom builds the house:
"By wisdom a house is built, and through understanding it is established."
(Proverbs 24:3)

Galileo is known to many as the "father of modern science." He was a professor of astronomy at the University of Pisa. He was a renaissance man of learning who famously deduced that the earth and the planets revolved around the Sun, rather than around the Earth as was commonly believed. Galileo's observations with his new telescope convinced him of the truth of Copernicus' sun-centred or heliocentric theory.

His beliefs got him into a lot of trouble with the Church of his day. In 1633 the Inquisition convicted him of heresy and forced him to publicly withdraw his support of Copernicus. They sentenced him to life imprisonment, but because of his advanced age allowed him serve his term under house arrest at his villa in Arcetri outside of Florence.

It sounds absurd doesn't it? But there were people a few centuries before Galileo who believed the world was also flat! One such man was Cosmas Indicopleustes.[58] He was a merchant traveller who retired to become a monk in the Egyptian desert where he wrote a treatise on Christian Topology that included his flat Earth cosmology. The book was widely ignored at the time and scholars of the day scoffed at his book as being the work of an uneducated fool – which it was! But Church at that time built a school of thought based upon his theology that was in error and persecuted those who thought differently.

Their philosophy and practice was all based on error – it sounds crazy to us now but it was true! But just as shocking to me is the thought that it is still possible for church leaders today to build something other than the Church as God intended *and* think in our hearts that we are building well! Many are building church based on erroneous philosophies and flawed theology. They think what they are doing is right and believe wholeheartedly in what they are building. They have deeply held convictions and are fully persuaded that they are right. This sounds worrying, I know, but it is possible for us to build something that looks like church, but has been built according to our plans, not God's.

Notice the words of Jesus in Luke 19:46:

> "It is written … 'My house will be a house of prayer'; *but you have made it* 'a den of robbers'."

The words, "but you have made …" are striking. Jesus is highlighting that the religious authorities of His day had turned His Father's house into something it was never intended to be. They had taken the original plans and totally distorted them. God's intent was that His house was to be a house of prayer, a house of connections, a house of salvation, of healing, of deliverance and power. God's original plan was that His house would be one of creativity and passion, where the lost could become "found". His house was intended to be a place where people would find grace and mercy, forgiveness and acceptance. But the religious leaders of the day "made it" into something else.

Is it just me or is it possible for "well meaning" religious people to highjack the supernatural process of building Church and construct something that is not the House of God? I think it is. This is a horrifying revelation. Are we following the plans of the Original Architect? Are we using the Master Plan? Are we in relationship with the Architect and following His every command? Are we co-labourers with Christ? Or have we, in fact, taken over the building site and stamped our own name on it, or that of our denomination?

We are not clones. Of course we won't all create "buildings" that have the same atmosphere and feel when you walk through the door. Our styles of worship and preaching will be different. The house we build for God will have its own unique personality. But the foundations – the mission and intent of the church – should be the same, no matter where we build it.[59]

Expert builders

Paul said in 1 Corinthians 3:9-11, "For we are God's fellow-workers; you are God's field, God's building. By the grace God has given me, I laid a foundation as an expert builder, and someone else is building on it. But each one should be careful how he builds. For no one can lay any foundation other than the one already laid, which is Jesus Christ."

We need to be careful how we build and persevere to become "expert builders" who are carefully working on the foundation laid down by Jesus. What does this mean in practice? If Christ is the foundation, then as expert builders we must understand the character and nature of this Person. It is vital we understand why He came and what He accomplished through His death and resurrection. We need desperately to acquaint ourselves with His mission and purpose. Then, with great care, we build upon this foundation.

Ephesians 2:19-22 is rich in its imagery about the master plan of the Church: "Consequently," Paul declares, "you are no longer foreigners and aliens, but fellow-citizens with God's people and members of God's household, built on the foundation of the apostles and prophets, with Christ Jesus himself as the chief cornerstone. In him the whole building is joined together and rises to become a holy temple in the Lord. And in him you too are being built together to become a dwelling in which God lives by his Spirit."

Our building blocks are people. Peter refers to us in 1 Peter 2:5 as being "… like living stones, being built into a spiritual house to be a holy priesthood, offering spiritual sacrifices acceptable to God through Jesus Christ." Therefore we need to be building people. We need to be training, developing and instructing people in how to live.

Notice the words "built" and "foundation." These words imply a plan and a master builder. Nobody tries to build a house without a plan and architect's drawings. We know who the Master Builder is. "In Him the whole building is joined together." He is the Master Designer, the Chief Cornerstone. "In Him you too are being built together to become a dwelling in which God lives by His Spirit." See the majesty, see the awesome nature of what He is building, see the emphasis He places upon us as living stones, full of His presence. I love this picture of the Church being filled with God.

Seeing examples

It's one thing to describe this awesome Church in words and another to see it working. I hope through this book you get a clear idea of what church should look like, but there is nothing like witnessing a thriving church that is touching its community, a city or even the world.

The Bible is full of examples and stories, and even letters written to other church leaders that can guide us. We have epistles such as Corinthians, which on the one hand brings correction to the Corinthian church, while on the other praises the generosity of the Macedonian church. But, thankfully, we also have thousands of live, working models – great churches that are significantly impacting their world. On every continent there are churches of influence that inspire us with their relentless pursuit of God and the mission of Christ. In every language and culture we see cutting edge churches "seeking and saving those who are lost." They are making an impact and producing excellent fruit.

Some churches have styles we don't get and their services are conducted in languages we can't understand. Some of these great churches have ways of doing things that don't necessarily gel with us and others have a theology we struggle with. We've seen churches that inspire us to bring change and to be more effective in touching our cities and others that we respect but can't work out. Some of these churches scare us because they're big, so we feel threatened and react negatively.

Some of these great churches are led by outstanding individuals who stir us, while others are led by very unassuming leaders who are so humble it makes you sick! When we compare these great churches with our own we can we feel either a bit small or insignificant or be inspired and see the benefits a new model could offer. When seeking to follow the Master's plan we don't need to fly by the seat of our pants. We don't need to work blind because there are great people out there to help and instruct us. There are many great examples of effective churches we can observe, we just need to look and see.

Sometimes it's just good to have a look at the other churches around us that are growing and impacting their community. I love the variety, I love the diversity, I love the mixture, and I love the different personalities and styles of these great churches and their leaders. Behold the multifaceted nature of God reflected in human personality. It is awe inspiring. You don't need to become a clone of someone else to build a successful and effective church, but we can draw inspiration from their example.

Standing on the shoulders of giants

The 12th century theologian and author John of Salisbury said in his treatise on logic called *Metalogicon* written in Latin in 1159, "We are like dwarfs sitting on the shoulders of giants. We see more, and things that are more distant, than they did, not because our sight is superior or because we are taller than they, but because they raise us up, and by their great stature add to ours."

God has used many and varied personalities to move forward His agenda. It is important for us to be connected with others who have achieved much in the kingdom so that even as "dwarfs" we can sit on their shoulders and "see more" because of their great stature. Instead of being intimidated or showing a grudging respect for others, should we not embrace and be influenced by them?

I believe there are many people strategically placed throughout the world who are there to demonstrate God's consummate genius. I believe it is not only vital for us to be connected to something bigger than ourselves, but vital to allow those influences to impact our own work for the kingdom.

I realised quickly on my return from the mission field that things in the Church had changed. What an understatement! Church wasn't being done the way I did church some thirteen years previously. It was definitely a lot different from the way we did it in Bangkok! A lot had changed and I owe a lot to a few friends who stood with me during the dark days of transition. One was Gary Clarke, Pastor of Hillsong London. I've known Gary for nearly twenty-five years and I was pleased he was now in London leading this exciting church.

In my first year of being in Norwich I made about 20 trips to London to check out what was happening there. I was awe struck. I saw the kind of church I wanted to pastor. During my brief visits I re-established my friendship with Gary and was soon catching the DNA of the Hillsong church. I saw the culture and how it was being built. I enjoyed the chance to see firsthand what was happening.

As I look back now, I can see that not only was it personally helpful to me to see Hillsong in action, but that a godly principle was at work:[60] we need both friends who are fellow builders and good models to learn from. We are not designed to do the job of leading a church in isolation. It is vital to have like-minded people around us to network with and generally bounce ideas off.

Some people are not good at this. They tend to be disingenuous towards others who are building successfully and, in the process, they damage themselves. Some leaders are too proud to go and see; others feel too intimidated to ask for a look or for help. Some leaders suffer from a lack of confidence and battle self-esteem issues so much that they would never engage in such a relationship in case they suffered further hurt.

But Proverbs 27:17 says, "As iron sharpens iron, so one man sharpens another."

If we want to learn, grow and develop ourselves then we need to place ourselves in a bigger world where others who are further ahead can speak to us and influence us. In order to build a thriving, influential church you as the leader must grow and be stretched and enlarged. Growing churches are led by growing leaders, so personal growth must always be a high priority.

What I saw in Hillsong was a church being built according to the original Architect's plans. I experienced an atmosphere and felt the passion. I saw a *working model* of a church in action, with good leadership, effective governance and a clear mission. I saw a church that was deliberately and intentionally being shaped, built and developed a certain way to have an impact by its senior leadership both in London and Australia. What I saw was an awesome church emerging in one of Europe's greatest cities! The church was strong, prophetic, powerful, effective, significant, influential and very exciting. I saw people connecting with Christ in salvation in every meeting I attended.

And it was BIG!

I knew that we in Norwich might not ever be as big as Hillsong London, or grow as quickly as they did, but I did know that we had to capture the "spirit" of this church that I was seeing demonstrated so ably. Every person has their own road to travel and my journey is different to Gary Clarke's. But here was an effective model for twenty-first century church: a church where people were coming to Christ in their hundreds on a weekly basis, where there existed a volunteer spirit second to none, where people were prepared to sacrifice their personal preferences and go with the flow, a church with a generosity that was astounding. It was mind boggling.

Proverbs 2:20 instructs us to, *"...walk in the ways of good men* and keep to the paths of the righteous." When David wrote this he was talking about much more than methodology. He is urging us to understand the ways and thought processes of good men who are following God's plan. We don't simply observe other leaders so that we can import their programmes, imitate their preaching styles or pinch their sermons! Instead we want to pick up their spirit, their attitudes, and their ways and culture. We need to learn how they move in the power of the Holy Spirit.

Personally, I wanted to find out not merely how things were done, but what things were implemented and why. Over time I began to understand the ingredients of the culture and how these were introduced into the mainstream life of the church.

Counting the cost to build according to the plan

Having spent the time to understand the type of church that I believed God wanted me to build, I had to ask myself a question. Was I willing to fight for what I believed? Did I really believe I was called of God and gifted by Christ as a pastor according to Ephesians 4:11? If so, was I prepared to take a stand to see this through to the end? Was I courageous enough?

It was an exercise in counting the cost. As Jesus Himself said,

> "Suppose one of you wants to build a tower. Will he not first sit down and estimate the cost to see if he has enough money to complete it? For if he lays the foundation and is not able to finish it, everyone who sees it will ridicule him, saying, 'This fellow began to build and was not able to finish." (Luke 14:28-30)

I first had to ensure that, within my own heart, my motivation for pursuing this course was pure. People around me told me that it would be a costly journey and some people would get hurt. I had to prayerfully consider whether this was a path I wanted to go down. Having a good model is great; having a fresh vision of the Church from Scripture is vital; to build according to the Architect's plan is essential; but was I willing to pay the price?

Not everyone is faced with similar circumstances to me, but here is the dilemma that every single leader must face: following the vision for the church God wants you to build *will* bring you into conflict with some people. People will disagree with you, you will be put under pressure to do things you don't want to do, and they will often oppose you. What do leaders do when this happens?

In the end it usually comes down to a "Joshua moment". Leaders frequently need to remind themselves who they are serving and then make a choice. As Joshua himself said, "If serving the Lord seems undesirable to you, then choose for yourselves this day whom you will serve" (Joshua 24:15).

Following the Master's plan allows for no shortcuts or corner cutting. To build what Christ wants to see will cost us our lives and require courage, risk-taking, wisdom, insight and discernment. I needed all of these in abundance for my own journey and in hindsight I wished I'd sought harder for them. But I love the courage of Joshua as he says, in answer to his own question, "… as for me and my household, we will serve the Lord" (Joshua 24:15).

When you make up your mind you're going to serve God and follow only the master plan, get ready for the most exciting ride of your life. In the words of Cypher from *The Matrix*[61], "Buckle your seatbelt, Dorothy, 'cause Kansas is going bye-bye!"

Building according to the Master's design will continue to require courage, foresight and, on some days, more energy than you've got. But in the end you will have the utter satisfaction of leading a church that is making permanent and eternal change in the world you live in.

The role of friends

My friends stood with me, prayed for me and were also a continual source of comic relief. In the darkest moments they helped me laugh and keep my sense of humour. Thank God for great friends who are willing to stand the ground with you.

It's not good to be an island. Walking by yourself is lonely and potentially dangerous. This may come as a shock, but you are not the repository of all wisdom! You need friends on the journey. You can be "the man", but you can't do it all on your own. The wisdom of Scripture regarding this principle is broad and deep:

"Wounds from a friend can be trusted, but an enemy multiplies kisses" (Proverbs 27:6). Not every time I met with my friends did they bless and encourage me. There were times when they spoke quite clearly and told me if I did this or that I was an idiot! They saved me from disaster time and time again.

"As iron sharpens iron, so one man sharpens another" (Proverbs 27:17). I love hanging out with people who sharpen me. I find I actually prepare myself for their visits too. It's exhilarating to be sharpened by others. We all need these kinds of people in our lives. They poke fun at us because sometimes we take things too seriously. One of my mates said to me, "Tom, you need to lighten up and learn to laugh at yourself – because everyone else is!"

"Perfume and incense bring joy to the heart, and the pleasantness of one's friend springs from his earnest counsel" (Proverbs 27:9). Many times I have called a friend to tell them what I'm thinking of doing and it was good to hear another perspective on my idea. I actively seek other points of view. It's good to get feedback from other leaders. Earnest counsel is invaluable.

We need good friends in our life as leaders. Proverbs 19:20 says, "Listen to advice and accept instruction, and in the end you will be wise." We don't have to go through everything on our own.

"Make plans by seeking advice; if you wage war, obtain guidance" (Proverbs 20:18). Be wise and choose some wise friends to walk through the big deals in your life. Remember, wisdom builds the house. Make a decision to not burn out, rust out or go out with a bang. You don't need to melt down if you walk the journey with good friends and wise advisors. One of my life-long mentors once told me to phone him whenever I needed because, "A five minute phone call could avert five years of disaster."

Oscar Wilde[62] once said, "True friends stab you in the front!" Bernard Meltzer[63] once said, "A true friend is someone who thinks that you are a good egg even though he knows you are slightly cracked." We need good friends!

I've met a lot of leaders who somehow feel it is good to be a Lone Ranger; that it is somehow a sign of weakness to ask for help or advice. They are wrong. A great leader can be measured by the number of other great leaders around him whom he counts as friends and trusted advisors. Great leaders meet with great leaders who challenge them, who move in larger spheres of influence. Their presence helps make us bigger on the inside.

Being a lifelong learner

To build according to the architect's plan we need to spend time reading and meditating in Scripture, and we need to spend time learning from great churches and church leaders. If we isolate ourselves and cut ourselves off from the many great networks that exist we will cut short this great restructuring of the Church. It is vital to be connected with others at various stages of growth. I have learned so much in the areas of leadership and structure from big churches, but equally I must demonstrate and pass on what I have learned so that it impacts growth and development of smaller churches. This causes multiplication and results in even greater growth for us and for others.

Gary McIntosh subtitled his book, *Taking Your Church to the Next Level*[64], with the words: "What got you here isn't going to take you there." In other words, the structures and systems employed to bring growth must change over time, otherwise we'll get stuck. If we want to reach a new level, we need to access God's strategy for it. The Church is a living organism, not an institution. This is why we must be lifelong learners. To go beyond our current level of growth will require us to connect with those who have gone before us, to stand on the shoulders of giants.

Our personal growth is a personal responsibility. Attending conferences and workshops will be invaluable; reading good books is priceless; asking another church leader out to lunch could change the way you see your church and inspire you to the next level; sitting down with a larger church's administrator could help you see things you would otherwise not have seen. Identifying yourselves with two or three strategic networks could also help. Get connected with a desire to see a big picture of the Master Plan. Stay connected with Jesus too. He is the Master Architect! We can learn from others, but never underestimate the power of revelation. Never underestimate your personal relationship with Jesus and the Holy Spirit.

I believe with all my heart it is Europe's time to flourish. To use an old fashion word I believe Europe is on the edge of a mighty all consuming revival of church planting and church growth. Because of its location in the world and ease of travel between nations, Europe is becoming better connected; friends and networking churches are rising everywhere and it is awesome to behold.

I believe with all my heart that God is stirring something new and fresh in the hearts of many pastors both young and old. I believe that we need a re-think on our theology of the Church. I believe it is time for a renaissance theology for the 21st Century Church to be emphasised in today's Church.

Notes

58. Encyclopaedia Britannica, 2008, Cosmas Indicopleustes
59. Ephesians 2:21-22
60. Jeremiah 1:3,13; 24:3
61. The Matrix, a cult 1999 US science fiction action movie that became hugely popular and questioned the reality of life as we know it.
62. Oscar Fingal O'Flahertie Wilde, an Irish author and poet
63. Bernard Meltzer, US radio host
64. Gary McIntosh, *Taking Your Church to the Next Level,* Baker Publishing Group, September 2009

4

A CHURCH IN YOUR CITY

"Setting an example is not the main means of influencing another, it is the only means."
—Albert Einstein

"Who shall set a limit to the influence of a human being?"
—Ralph Waldo Emerson

"Every block of stone has a statue inside it and it is the task of the sculptor to discover it."
—Michelangelo

"In everything set them an example by doing what is good."
(Titus 2:7)

In 1504 Michelangelo concluded work on one of his most famous works of art: the statue of David. Traditionally, David was portrayed holding Goliath's head after the battle, but Michelangelo sought to show something different and portrayed David *before* the battle. David is seen looking tense and ready for battle, both physically and mentally. His slingshot is hardly noticeable, emphasising that David's victory was not based on sheer force, but upon his faith in God. It is a piece that shows the genius of Michelangelo, who extracted such beauty and symmetry from a piece of granite.

Many believe Michelangelo was inspired by God to produce this great work. I agree. We read of a similar "divine inspiration" in the book of Acts. One night Jesus spoke to the Apostle Paul in a vision about a church that was to be built in the city of Corinth – a church envisioned in the heart of Christ in eternity and revealed to the Apostle in time. It launched Paul into action and the result was a church that had a significant influence on its world.

"One night the Lord spoke to Paul in a vision: 'Do not be afraid; keep on speaking, do not be silent. For I am with you, and no one is going to attack and harm you, because I have many people in this city." (Acts 18:9-10)

Getting a vision for what your church can be in your city, town or village …

Historically, Corinth was a wicked, godless city. Its people possessed the Greek love of philosophical subtleties, but their immorality was notorious even in the pagan world. To "Corinthianize" someone became an expression that meant to wilfully corrupt a person with immorality. The highest deity or Corinth was Aphrodite (or Venus), the goddess of licentiousness. Worship at the temple of Aphrodite was attended with shameless and dissolute indulgence, with 1,000 female slaves being maintained for the service of strangers.

Yet, despite it being the most godless city in the Roman Empire, it was here that Paul began a church that would become an awesome force with a passionate heart for Europe. Interestingly, Norwich was voted the UK's most godless city after the 2001 UK census! Europe is today is one of the darkest places on earth. Europe once the hotbed of revival is now in the clutches darkness, the like of which it has never seen before. But that also makes it one of the world's greatest mission fields.

Your city, wherever you are in the world, needs Jesus. A large percentage of your city has no meaningful relationship with Christ and doesn't even know they can have a relationship with God. Many have never heard of Jesus or touched a Bible, much less read one. They are completely unaware of the fact the Jesus is alive and earnestly desires a relationship with them. These are the exact conditions that met Paul and his band of church planters when they came to Corinth.

Europe is now post modern, post Christian (maybe even pre-Christian!) absolutely godless and loving it! The new European constitution doesn't even mention God. Europe, once the light to the world, now lies in spiritual ruin. But God's Word has a message for us who seek to become prevailing, impacting and effective churches:

"Don't be afraid " – a *confident* Church is emerging!

Across the continent, right in the heart of European towns and cities, a new Church is emerging. It is a Church full of faith in God and what He can do; a Church that is vibrant, passionate and audacious; a fearless Church and a church with attitude!

Where once we saw the impotency of fear we are now seeing the power of confidence in God. The word confidence, from its biblical roots, denotes an attitude that is "in your face." It is not arrogance, but rather has supreme assurance that the One who promises to do something is more than able to do it. Some may view such assurance as brash or cocky, maintain that the Church should be humble and meek, but Scripture does not bear this out. We should not return to the militancy of some former movements and ride rough shod over people, but we need to be "biblically confident". Biblical confidence is being sure about what God has said to you – about you, your gifts, your talents and your destiny. It is a holy boldness, vigour and assertiveness – the kind of confidence that is risk taking, creative, entrepreneurial and intensive.

Impotence, the opposite of boldness, is one of the strongholds over Europe that needs to be broken. In many places churches are portraying a limp brand of Christianity. They may have a vision, but are powerless to achieve it. There remains a sense of helplessness and incapacity because of this spiritual impotence. Many churches are limp because of what they believe about themselves. They lack passion and desire and are afraid to push forward. Never in the history of the Church has there been a greater need for courageous leadership as today. I read a tweet on Twitter the other day that said, "If no one is following you, all you're doing is typing." How true! Put another way, he who leads but has no one following merely taketh a walk!

The picture of leadership in the Bible is characterised by the Middle Eastern shepherd who leads his sheep from the front, calling them by name as he leads them to green pastures. It's such a contrast from the picture of the Australian shepherd I grew up with, who gets his Blue Healer dogs to nip and bark and run rough shod over the sheep. For a boy it was fun to watch a dog actually run over the heads and bodies of the sheep, herding them in the direction he wanted them to go, but the dog frightened the sheep in order to drive them into the pen.

Godly leadership and Christ's gifting must be exercised with grace and love with wisdom as its crowning glory! The Church is crying out for leadership empowered by the Holy Spirit – men and women anointed by God with true gifts of Christ within them, who will walk with wisdom, insight, and discernment to lead God's people into His blessing. We need confident, godly leadership.

Hebrews 13:6 also encourages us: "So we say with confidence, 'The Lord is my helper; I will not be afraid. What can man do to me?'" When we are creating a church culture we must be like those the writer of Hebrews is talking about. We need to create a language of communication that effectively describes what we want to achieve and take time to explain how it will happen. There is no need to frighten or nip, bark or bite the sheep into submission. They need to follow you because they see the gift of God within you.

Jesus told Paul not to be afraid and this fearless confidence is a sign of a new church emerging. Those who lead these new breed churches are fearless and relentless because they want only to see the will of God achieved in their church and in their city and in their nation.

Churches have destiny. Your church has a destiny! I know this is challenging, but it is supposed to be. We need courageous leadership to rise up in a spirit of relentless energy.

"Don't be silent" – a new Church with a *voice* and a *message!*

A new church is emerging with a voice! Oh, the tragedy of a silent church. No longer should the saying, "Silent as a church mouse" have any connection with the Church! Instead, Jesus promised the Apostle a church with a voice and a message and He makes the same promise to us.

The phrase "Be still" is found seven times in Scripture, but "shout" is found sixty-one times! Our mission in the earth is to "proclaim" or preach, not to keep silent. As in the Message's translation of Matthew 5, "we're going public with this!" Front page churches are rising with a voice and something solid to say.

The new Church that is emerging is motivated by a mission, the cause of Christ, and speaks with more than words. We are a people with something to say to our cities. We have a message that can transform others. We are a Church of significance that influences culture with lives that resound with the goodness of God. There are great relationships and friendships, marriages that last, children who love God and keep on loving God through their teens and on into their adult lives. The new, emerging church's people are living *attractive* lives, lives that smile, lives that are brave, resilient, passionate, strong and compelling; lives that speak a positive message, that are prosperous, that are positive and affirming, that have a contagious optimism, that are successful and full of faith. I hear the sound of a generation rising and they are loud!

The message of our Church is too important to be left to default. Our message to society needs to shout that it is life-changing, powerful and outstanding. Our churches should be houses of WOW! People should get a glimpse of Heaven when they come in, but for this to happen the communication of our message must be planned, purposeful and intentional.

All over our cities and towns every week the Holy Spirit is prompting people to go to church. The truth is that most people make up their minds within fifteen minutes of entering the building whether they are coming back or not. God has done His part. We must do ours. We must do everything we can do so that He can do what only He can do. This is why we are called upon by God to become the "architects" of a culture that will shout out His fame. We must build a culture that truly embraces those who are seeking after God.

"I am with you" – a Church with the *abiding presence* of God is emerging!

There is no greater architect of church culture than the Holy Spirit. We have no greater senior partner than Him. God is excited about our churches and desires them to grow. His desire is far greater than our own! Jesus said to Peter in Matthew 18 that He would build His Church. Jesus is smack dab in the middle of building His Church and we need to honour His presence and actively work with Him.

In the Acts 18 scripture we read earlier, one of the most important things we find is that Jesus says He is with us! Jesus is talking about a Church that knows His presence and as a result knows the favour of God. Is it even possible to have a church where Jesus is not present? The answer to that question becomes heartbreakingly clear as we read Revelation 3:20. This letter from Jesus is addressed to the leader of the church of Laodicea. Jesus said to him, "Behold I stand at the door and knock, if any man will open the door I will come in!"[65] Jesus speaks from the *outside* of a church, asking the senior leader if He can come in – if he / she will open the door to His personal presence.

By implication, yes, it is very possible to "do church" without Jesus. It is absurd, but true. This is how such a scenario as Luke 19:46 can occur: "My house will be a house of prayer ... but you have made it a den of robbers." Jesus has specific intentions for God's house, but we can "make it" into something He never wanted it to be, thwarting God's original design. The word "den" in the original Greek means "a cave" or "a place of refuge". The Church was never meant to be a "refuge" in the sense that it is cut off and insulated from the big bad world, living in ignorant serenity. No, we are meant to be "in the world", just not "worldly".

Jesus was clear about the Church's purpose: we are a city on a hill. We are meant to "attract" people's attention and draw them to us. As Wesley said, we are "a soul-saving station on the edge of Hell." We must be a Church that is prepared to bring all sorts of people into our midst to encounter God's presence; to be a Church that pursues the lost to see them come into relationship with Him.

The greatest sign that Jesus' presence is with us is that people are coming to Christ for salvation. I speak to many church leaders and hear this story repeatedly: many go months and some even years without seeing a single person come to salvation. Churches remain static in size and from year to year and no new members join. There is only one reason a church is in a community and that reason is to win the lost to Christ! Jesus said it so clearly: we are here to be a light to the world and salt to the earth. Seeing the lost find Christ is the main criterion that validates the existence of our churches. If your church is not winning people to Jesus then you are no more than a religious club. Harsh, but true.

It is an awful thing to sense that the presence of God has departed from you and that activities that were once filled with His life are now routine and empty. It is heartbreaking to realise that much of what you've done over the last season was just "going through the motions". It comes as a shock to discover that the Holy Spirit hasn't been active in regeneration and imparting new life because our services are all internally focused. In Craig Groeschel's great book, *IT*, he challenges to ask ourselves whether we have lost "it" and if so, how to get "it" back. The question must be asked and answered: are people getting saved and connecting with God? If not, then something vital is missing. We desperately need a Church where God manifests Himself in power and glory and the main outworking of this is the salvation of souls.

There is no one more passionate to see a godly culture develop in your church than the Holy Spirit, so work with Him. If you ask He will give you creative ideas and help you build a culture that will become irresistible. If you want to connect with people and be relevant, His presence is the starting point. The Holy Spirit can impart to you the wisdom to know what to change, when to change, what issues need dealing with and how to confront them. The Holy Spirit is our constant companion and if we cooperate with Him with grace and confidence we will win the hearts of many.

Craig Groeschel has also said, "I'm thrilled so many leaders are placing less emphasis on being cool and more emphasis on being like Christ." I agree.

"No one is going to harm you" – a *victorious* Church is emerging!

The new Church that is emerging is full of overcoming people who know their God; a Church where it's okay to succeed and be prosperous and not apologise for it; a Church where it's okay to smile, be happy and enjoy life, including having fun in church and being passionate in worship. This new Church has a culture of significance and greatness – a culture that cares very little where you have come from and believes passionately that God has a greater future for you; a Church that works intentionally to foster wholeness and brings people to maturity in Christ.

Victory, success and prosperity are biblical concepts. God told Joshua,

"Be strong and courageous, because you will lead these people to inherit the land I swore to their forefathers to give them. Be strong and very courageous. Be careful to obey all the law my servant Moses gave you; do not turn from it to the right or to the left, that you may be successful wherever you go. Do not let this Book of the Law depart from your mouth; meditate on it day and night, so that you may be careful to do everything written in it. Then you will be prosperous and successful. Have I not commanded you? Be strong and courageous. Do not be terrified; do not be discouraged, for the LORD your God will be with you wherever you go." (Joshua 1:6-9)

In 3 John 2 we read the Apostle John's prayer that we would, "… prosper and be in good health, just as your soul prospers." What a great concept. What a sound and encompassing word for

God's people – prosperity of soul! As we model it, live it and teach others how to live it, the culture of the church will become victorious and healthy, successful and full of fun!

With success and greatness comes a church that knows *victory* – a victory that shows in our lives, on our faces and in our spirits; a victory others see and want. God is the God of victory in many areas of our lives:

> *We have victory over the Devil:* "I have given you authority to trample on snakes and scorpions and to overcome all the power of the enemy; nothing will harm you." (Luke 10:19)

> *We are victorious over our enemies:* "But the wicked will perish: The Lord's enemies will be like the beauty of the fields, they will vanish, vanish like smoke" (Psalm 37:20).

> *We are victorious over the strongholds established by our enemies:* "For though we live in the world, we do not wage war as the world does. The weapons we fight with are not the weapons of the world. On the contrary, they have divine power to demolish strongholds. We demolish arguments and every pretension that sets itself up against the knowledge of God, and we take captive every thought to make it obedient to Christ" (2 Corinthians 10:3-5).

> *We have victory even in trials and tribulations:* Circumstances will conspire against us, but Jesus said in John 16:33, "I have told you these things, so that in me you may have peace. In this world you will have trouble. But take heart! I have overcome the world."

> *God has promised us victory in life:* "No, in all these things we are more than conquerors through him who loved us" (Romans 8:37).

> All of this leads to us being a victorious Church: "I will build my church, and the gates of Hades will not overcome it" (Matthew 16:18).

But we must get ready for opposition, as the powers of Hell will oppose any church where people are coming to Christ. Fortunately, we know that their opposition cannot stand. Isaiah 54:17 tell us, "'No weapon forged against you will prevail, and you will refute every tongue that accuses you. This is the heritage of the servants of the LORD, and this is their vindication from me,' declares the LORD." Weapons will be formed and accusations made, but God Himself will fight for us. No weapon will prevail and God will ultimately vindicate you.

By faith we need to conquer our fears and go out into the world with the power of God's Spirit upon us. We need to fan into flame the gift of God within us and do mighty exploits for Him. We need to be the forerunners of this new, fearless and victorious Church, destined for greatness with success assured because the favour of God rests on her.

"I have *many* people in this city" – a *large* Church is emerging!

I make no apologies for saying I believe the new Church that is emerging will be large! We see signs of it already in the world as much larger churches than we are used to seeing in the West are rising up and occupying positions of influence in their cities and nations.

Jesus said to Paul, "I have many people in this city!" and He says the same thing about all of our cities. We know what "many" means: a large indefinite number, numerous, much, a lot, bountiful, copious, plentiful … Have you got the picture yet? God says about your city that He has *many* people in it. It is our ministry to reach them. God desires your church to be BIG!

I believe God is calling for a prevailing Church to arise in Europe, a Church that is forever expanding, always developing, continually visioning, always reaching out to the lost and those in need. I sense God is asking us to be a people who are touching the untouchable in our world; to be a church that desires to see people connecting with Christ regularly and sees the majority of its growth through people becoming Christians. The new Church that is emerging has its eyes on the unsaved and its heart towards the un-churched.

"Many" means a constant supply of new preachers, new worship leaders, new pastors, new workers and many more leaders and volunteers in our city! Most of the people who will occupy these roles in the near future don't even know they are marked by destiny yet, but they are! The greatest preachers have yet to find their voices and the greatest churches are yet to be built in Europe and around the world.

In March 2006 I attended a strategic leadership conference, hosted by Mal Fletcher, entitled *The Church 2020*. I came away from that conference with this ringing in my spirit:

> "The future for the Church is bright. Europe and her desperate desire to flee from the light of the Gospel will be overshadowed by hundreds of 'mega churches'."

I believe that the future of the "large" Church is assured.

Notes

65. Revelation 3:20

5

WHAT DO YOU REALLY BELIEVE?

Keep away from those who try to belittle your ambitions. Small people always do that, but the really great make you believe that you too can become great.
—Mark Twain

What matters is not the idea a man holds, but the depth at which he holds it.
—Ezra Pound

Only believe, only believe; All things are possible, only believe
—Lyrics by Paul Rader

"Jesus looked at them and said, 'With man this is impossible, but not with God; all things are possible with God.'"
(Mark 10:27)

Of all the leaders of the contemporary Church in our world, whenever you hear Brian Houston speak you know that you are listening to a man who loves the Church and places great value on it. You soon realise that he believes everything he says about the majesty and wonder of the Church, both worldwide and in every local situation. I pay tribute to Brian because of the thousands of speakers I have heard over the last thirty years he stands out as one whose emphasis has always been "…to champion the cause of the local church."

What do you really believe?

What we *really believe* ultimately becomes our experience. What we believe, deep down, about the Church will set its boundaries in our city, town or village. It's not what we would *like* to believe, nor what we've been *taught* to believe that matters, or even our current theological position, but our deeply held, intrinsic beliefs and personal convictions. These are what will steer our experience.

Jesus put it this way: "For out of the overflow of the heart the mouth speaks" (Matthew 12:34). If you want to know what people really believe, listen to them speaking in an unguarded moment! What we truly believe will cross our lips eventually.

Thinking about my own city of Norwich, for examples, some leaders I speak to say, "Our city is a hard place." That is their deeply held belief and that is exactly what the city becomes for them. Some make mention of the prevalence of witchcraft and other occult practices and make the assumption that it must be hard to win people to Jesus in such an atmosphere.

Theologically we may believe in the resurrection of Christ[66] and His absolute defeat of the devil[67], sin and death[68]. We may believe that whoever calls on the name of the Lord will be saved[69]. But deep down we may also attribute power to the devil to hinder us and the message of Christ, instead of holding the deep conviction that there is an open heaven over our city.[70] We may believe this is a tough, hard place for the Gospel, instead of believing that people are just as hungry for spiritual reality and divine purpose here as anywhere else,[71] that they will go to extraordinary lengths to find God.[72] Either way we will perform according to what we actually believe.

The Bible confirms this principle of beliefs driving our speech and our actions. 2 Corinthians 4:13 says, "It is written: 'I believed; therefore I have spoken.' With that same spirit of faith we also believe and therefore speak." We will say and do what we believe to be true, even if it is out of line with Scripture. That is why believing in the "right things" is vital if we are going to build Church according to the Master Builder's design! We cannot base our beliefs solely on what our denomination says about the Church, or what our experience has taught us about the Church. We may have been taught that the Church will always be a small, struggling entity – a band of a few faithful followers hanging on until Christ returns to save us. And if you believe that deep down, then you will consistently justify that as the reason why your church is small and insignificant. But such a belief would be completely out of line with the truth of the Bible!

Alternatively, if you believe it is the Church's responsibility to judge modern society and culture then you will never understand the power of being "a light to the world." If you feel the Church's role in society is to let the world know that we disagree with them by signing petitions and picketing, then you'll never understand the power of "bringing out the God-colours and God-flavours" in the world around you.

Take some time out to examine carefully what you actually believe, what you fundamentally hold as true. These convictions are the ones that are shaping the church you lead. One way or another, what you believe you speak into reality. For this reason, I hope you will find this section of this book important and helpful. Here we will look at foundational scriptures in a fresh light and, I hope, challenge some deeply held but erroneous beliefs. Put bluntly, I want to confront some of the rubbish that gets spoken about the Church! I want us, together, to understand what the Bible is really saying about the Church, beyond those beliefs that come from our personal experiences or our denomination's rhetoric. I hope together we will barbeque some of those sacred cows! "These sacred cows trample creativity and stamp out innovative thinking. They roam everywhere – in halls, boardrooms and offices and in people's minds.[73]"

Take seriously the words of the Apostle when he says, "With that *same spirit of faith* we also believe and therefore speak." Listen to the Word of God as it describes the Church. Listen to the Original Designer as He speaks about His Church. With the same spirit of faith, catch the vision of the Master Planner and see yourself working with Him as you build the Church of His dreams. What you believe about the Church is what kind of church you will build. If your belief structure about the Church is faulty, then you will build a faulty church foundation. But if you have a clear and purposeful understanding of what Jesus is building then you will find yourself as a co-labourer with Him following the original design.

What the Bible says about the Church

The word "church" is exclusively a New Testament word. The Greek is *ekklesia* (ek-klay-see'-ah) from which we derive our English word "ecclesiastical". The doctrine of the Church in theological terms is called *ecclesiology*. The word *ekklesia* appears 80 times in Scripture to describe the Church.

Essentially *ekklesia* means "a calling out". Its context in Scripture is always that of "people", not a "place" – a people "called out" by God to be unique and separate. As well as being "a church" it could equally be translated "an assembly" and applies to both the local and universal Church. There were no church buildings for at least the first 300 years of the Church. The concept of our modern church building would have been foreign to early believers. What was important was that the Church was a community of people, chosen and anointed by God for service.[74]

We are "called out ones" because we are a people called to belong to Christ and build our lives upon the same confession that Peter made: "You are the Christ, the Son of the living God![75]" This confession is what separates us from others – our belief and recognition of Christ as Messiah, God's only Son, Redeemer and Saviour. We are a people who recognise His kingdom rule and Lordship. Peter writes in 1 Peter 2:10, "Once you were not a people, but now you are the people of God; once you had not received mercy, but now you have received mercy."

The size and significance of the Church
Size

In the NIV Bible there are nineteen direct references to the Church in the book of Acts alone. These are exciting Scriptures that reflect the nature of the Church in those first few decades.

Acts 2:41-47 says, "Those who accepted his message were baptised, and about three thousand were added to their number that day; they devoted themselves to the apostles' teaching and to the fellowship, to the breaking of bread and to prayer. Everyone was filled with awe, and many wonders and miraculous signs were done by the apostles."

Such verses encourage us that expansive church growth is possible, but many today are asking the question: how big should a church be?

In Acts we get a glimpse of the dynamic nature and significance of the Church. We get an idea of how big Jesus thought His church should be. There were 3,000 members on the first day and a few weeks later the congregation was recorded as 5,000 men, so with women and children it was nearer 20,000 strong. Church history tells us the Jerusalem Church was over 100,000 strong. In other words, the church was a powerful force in the city. A "significant" church had been born. God was giving us a glimpse of what He intended for His Church.

The early Church grew and more people were converted by the preaching of God's Word by His messengers, preachers and teachers. It was never God's intention that the size of His church would be capped or become static, or indeed lose members or that its growth would lose momentum. The plan of God was that the Church would be dynamic, ever increasing in size and always prevailing.

So why are there so many different sizes of church? Why do some churches struggle to thrive and grow? I believe the answer comes back to leadership. Every leader has a personal capacity and individual ability. Jesus put it this way in Matthew 25:15: "To one he gave five talents of money, to another two talents, and to another one talent, each according to his ability."

It should come as no surprise that the global average size of church is 65 people. Why? Because that's what one person can manage. It is a size where everyone can know everyone else and the church feels comfortable.

Why do certain leaders have a church that grows to around 250 members, but after a year or so shrinks back to 150 members (substitute any number you want here)? The size of the membership is proportional to the capacity/ability of the leader(s). Churches will grow to a point where the leaders are no longer able to manage the growth and begin losing ground. People will still continue to connect with Jesus and get saved, but after a while, more experienced believer will become frustrated with the status quo, get upset and "feel that the Lord is moving us on" or not attend as much as they used to.

This is challenging, but the story doesn't finish here. Notice the guy with five talents in Jesus' parable. Applying it to a leadership paradigm, here is a man who works hard to reproduce himself through wise investment and he turns his "five" into "ten" – doubling the size of his church. As we commit to personal growth and help to grow those around us, so our capacity for further growth increases. I also like the fact that as this guy's capacity reached ten talents, his master just added an extra one because he was faithful in his commitment to growth. God gives us an unexpected blessing simply because we work hard at increasing our capacity!

Significance

The day of Pentecost was so much more than a supernatural spectacle, though it was certainly that. It was a description and a "prescription" of what the Church should be. Pentecost was supernatural, violent, full of fire and outwardly focused. This group of people didn't start a movement to display their theological correctness, they spoke to the gathered crowd passionately, full of the Holy Spirit, and declared the message of salvation. They lifted high the name of Jesus and preached Christ and His resurrection. They were bold, daring, audacious and relentless! And their message had an impact.

Acts 2:37-38 says, "When the people heard this, they were cut to the heart and said to Peter and the other apostles, 'Brothers, what shall we do?' Peter replied, 'Repent and be baptised, every one of you, in the name of Jesus Christ for the forgiveness of your sins. And you will receive the gift of the Holy Spirit.'

Men's hearts were cut to the quick and the early Church was birthed with thousands responding to the message. Many in the Church today seem afraid of the Holy Spirit. They fear being labelled "weird" or don't want identify themselves with certain kinds of revival. But the fact is, it was the power of the Holy Spirit alone that took the Church from being a small assembly in an upper room to the main streets of Jerusalem, and from there to the uttermost parts of the earth.

The early Church was full of people who exhibited growth in their personal lives and knew what it meant to be a "disciple". The Bible describes how they enacted the will of God by the way they lived and grew in the fruits of the Spirit. People used their spiritual gifts to reach out to others and heal them. They manifested the life of God to others and this led dynamically and directly to more salvations. These early Christians were not spectators, but active participants who used what God had given them to reach others for Christ and influence their culture.

In Acts 8 we read that persecution arose and when the believers were scattered from Jerusalem, they spread out everywhere proclaiming Christ as Messiah. They planted churches wherever the Holy Spirit directed them and their influence and significance continued to grow. Some of the leaders of the Church were imprisoned for preaching the message of Jesus Christ, which was viewed as heresy by local religious leaders. Some paid the ultimate price and were martyred for the name of Christ. But the significance of the movement continued to grow.

These Christian pioneers and leaders moved with great spiritual power, especially in the realm of healing the sick and casting out evil spirits. It is recorded in Acts that even if Peter's shadow fell across a sick person they were healed, and Paul sent out handkerchiefs to the sick to minister healing and release them from the powers of the occult.

Infused with such spiritual power the Church grew incredibly, despite intense persecution. But, from the time of Constantine until the reformation, the Church has seen many dark patches. Add to these 500 years of "reformation" and 150 years of "fundamentalism", "Pentecostalism," "the Charismatic Movement," and various weird and wonderful revivals of the late 20th century and early 21st century and, let's face it, we have become confused about what exactly the Church is and should be.

I firmly believe that the "vintage Church" of Acts should in fact be the Church of today. 2,000 years of Church history has blurred our vision and, like never before, we need to recapture Jesus' intentions for His Body. We must reject the unclear, hazy pictures of Jesus represented by many contemporary churches, set aside many unhelpful Church traditions that have become ingrained over the centuries, and discard the doubtful images of Christ represented by fashion and popular culture.

Let's spend some time back in Scripture looking a little closer at what the Church is and should be. It is vital we really understand the Architect's plans.

No "Plan B"

God the Holy Spirit is the Chief Executive Officer of Heaven and He is reviving the Church in these days. There is no doubt about it. People all over the world have a sense of revival in their hearts. Especially here in Europe, the Spirit is moving and the Church of Jesus Christ is rising! The people of God are willing to do "whatever it takes" and are committed to seeing God's name made famous and the influence of His kingdom affecting their cities and beyond.

The Holy Spirit is being poured out in abundance upon the Church. The Church is the hope of the world because God has *no other agency* He will use to reach out to a lost and dying world. God has no "Plan B" to employ in the event of the Church failing in its mission. Though there are many great "para-Church" organisations doing good work in the world, these are not God's backup plan being rolled out or a replacement for the Church. If the Church is in trouble, failing in its mission, God will do everything in His power to raise it up again, to renew it, to pour out His Spirit afresh and restore it. If necessary, God will create a "new breed" to inject new life and energy – and this is what He is doing.

There are signs of God doing this throughout history. In various generations revivals have taken place to bring the Church back to His original intentions. God's answer to a languishing Church is to raise up visionary leaders to spearhead another breakthrough for the Church. But building an awesome church doesn't just happen! Great care is needed as we seek to understand how the Church is meant to work. We need to make sure that as Jesus builds His church we, His people, are found doing whatever it takes to work with Him and not get in the way.

David wrote, "Unless the Lord builds the house, its builder's labour in vain. Unless the Lord watches over the city, the watchmen stand guard in vain." (Psalm 127:1)

Let's settle this fact from the very beginning: it is God who builds the house. We are his co-labourers. We help, but at the end of the day it is God who builds His house His way. Let's not labour in vain building something other than that which God intends! We want to be effective in our work.

Paul, the great Church architect, wrote, "I planted the seed, Apollos watered it, but God made it grow. So neither he who plants nor he who waters is anything, but only God, who makes things grow." (1 Corinthians 3:6-7)

Remember it is God who makes things grow. We can try all kinds of things to promote church growth, but in the end it is God who makes things grow. We can scratch around the ground, use fertilizers and even water the plants, but it is the seed that contains the miraculous ingredient called "life" and growth comes from within the seed. As Acts 2:47 says, "… *the Lord* added to their number daily those who were being saved."

People don't come to Christ because of some slick advertising campaign or because we have great musicians and cutting edge technology. People don't commit themselves to Him because we have a cool church that is culturally relevant. People respond to Christ because of the work of the Holy Spirit. People respond because He draws men and women to Christ and convicts them of sin, righteousness and judgment. People are born again because of the seed of the Word of God. A miracle takes place in their hearts that supernaturally converts them from a life of futility to a life of purpose and relationship with the God of the universe. Salvation is a work of God. There is nothing we mortals can do to save one single soul. But we can create an atmosphere where the Holy Spirit can move easily. We can engineer an environment and create a culture where the Holy Spirit is free to move and do those things that only He can do.

Titus 3:4-7 says it this way, "But when the kindness and love of God our Saviour appeared, he saved us, not because of righteous things we had done, but because of his mercy. *He saved us through the washing of rebirth and renewal by the Holy Spirit*, whom he poured out on us generously through Jesus Christ our Saviour, so that, having been justified by his grace, we might become heirs having the hope of eternal life."

Miraculously, God gives us the opportunity and privilege to build with Him as long as we see ourselves as co-labourers and Him as Master Builder and Architect! We're not trying to build something for ourselves or building according to our personal preferences.

Paul says in 1 Corinthians 3:8-11, "For *we are God's fellow workers; you are God's field, God's building*. By the grace God has given me, I laid a foundation as an expert builder, and someone else is building on it. But *each one should be careful how he builds*. For no one can lay any foundation other than the one already laid, which is Jesus Christ."

Let us never forget that we are fellow labourers with Christ. It is not us who build but HIM. He said He would build His Church and the gates of Hades would never prevail against it. It is "God's building" and each one of us are called upon by the Apostle to "be careful *how* we build."

Notes

66. Romans 4: 25
67. Romans 16: 20
68. 1 Corinthians 15: 55 – 58
69. Romans 10: 13
70. Malachi 3: 10
71. Ecclesiastes 3: 11 Amplified Bible
72. Luke 19:1–10
73. Kriegel and Brandt, *Sacred Cows Make the Best Hamburgers*, Harper Business, 1996.
74. 1 Peter 2: 9
75. Matthew 16: 16

6

THE CENTRALITY OF THE CHURCH

"Peripheral" – definition: concerned with relatively minor, irrelevant, or superficial aspects of the subject in question; of minor relevance or importance"
—Dictionary.com

"The church, you see is not peripheral to the world: the world is peripheral to the church. The church is Christ's body, in which he speaks and acts, by which he fills everything with his presence."
(Ephesians 1:22–23 The Message)

The word peripheral means "marginal, nonessential or secondary". I like the way that the above scripture in The Message Bible homes in on this essential truth about the Church. The world frequently sees the Church as *peripheral* to society. But seen from God's perspective it is absolutely *central!* It is the world that is peripheral to the Church! The Church is central to everything on Earth, not just to the religious world, but to the whole world, to our purpose, our lives, our destiny. Though the world does not realise it, the presence of the Church is essential; it is key to every aspect of government and significant to society. It is impossible to overstate its importance.

The NIV translates this scripture in this manner: "And God placed all things under his feet and appointed him to be head over everything for the church, which is his body, the fullness of him who fills everything in every way." (Ephesians 1:22-23)

When we realise that all things are under Christ's feet it empowers our prayers to, "Let your kingdom come and your will be done, on Earth as it is in Heaven." We need, by faith and wisdom, to bring the supremacy of Christ to bear upon the Earth, to declare that *everything* is and must come under His authority.

Paul writes that Jesus is "head over everything for the church." It speaks of Christ's pre-eminence, His sovereignty and His control over everything concerning the Church. It reminds us, especially those who lead churches, that we are co-labourers with Christ. Our job is to see what He wants done and work alongside Him to achieve it, not to wrestle control from His hands and build according to our own agenda and personal preferences.

I ask my congregation to pray for me regularly. They ask, "How should we pray?" My answer is simple: pray that I will hear the voice of the Lord speaking to me every day and in every situation. I need to hear His voice if I am to lead the way He wants me to lead, because He is head over all things concerning the church. I need that vital connection; I need to hear His voice.

It is good to remind ourselves constantly of the profound value that God has placed on the Church. He has positioned it at the centre of our universe. There is nothing more important, more priceless to Him than the Church – as a whole and as expressed in every local gathering. We need to be reminded of this truth for one good reason: how can we hope to achieve all that God has for us, both individually and corporately, if we don't believe the Church is central to God's plan in the Earth (and, by implication, that He will provide the power to back us up)? If we are sucked into the lie that the Church is peripheral to society, then we will never believe for or see a church that impacts its community, influencing lives, and reaching beyond to touch a nation.

We need, therefore, to come into alignment with God's thinking. We need to believe what He declares to be true and "see what He sees" concerning the Church. In Psalm 145:13 we read,

> "Your kingdom is an everlasting kingdom, and your dominion endures through all generations. The LORD is faithful to all his promises and loving towards all he has made."

The context here is Christ's authority. This understanding is linked with His Great Commission to the Church: "All authority in heaven and earth has been given to me, therefore go." When the psalmist speaks of an "everlasting kingdom" he envisages an eternal procession and progression of God's people, expressed through the Church, that flows out of Christ's authority and supremacy. The Church is Christ's body in and through which He speaks and acts, and by which He fills everything with His presence. He is the prevailing presence of the Church – not you or me, not our denomination!

The presence of Christ in His people is what now invades the world. We are a force; we are the pervading sense of the presence of God in the world today. The bigger any church becomes in a particular city, town or village, the more significant and impacting God's presence will be in that area. This is why I believe God desires His Church to be large and constantly growing! We need to be big so that we can impact big areas!

It is because "the Church is Christ's body, in which He speaks" that we see the Church as absolutely central to God's plans and everything else as peripheral. There is no Plan B! We look to the Church to hear what God is expressing through His body. When people look at the Church, they need to be able to see what Jesus is like. We are "the" expression of Him on the Earth! This is not something that is expressed from the platform only, but is seen in the lives of church members – how they live, what they say, how they treat one another and relate to those outside the church. First impressions are usually deep and lasting, so we want to be a people who "impress" others as being honest and accurate reflections of our Master.

Some time ago a very controversial play was put on and performed at our local playhouse. It was filled with blasphemy and expletives. The local church community was up in arms over it and a group of them decided they were going to picket the theatre. During the course of their protests they were rude to patrons of the theatre, caused an obstruction as they tried to block entry to the theatre, and generally made a nuisance of themselves.

During the week I was approached by a minister asking if our church would come and picket along with them. I politely declined the invitation, saying that we wanted to be known for what we were *for* rather than what we were *against*. My minister friend and I had to agree to disagree.

The next day I decided to call the Director of the theatre. I asked him how he was fairing with my minister friends: was he okay, no bruises or broken bones? He laughed and said he was holding up quite well. I then told him that I would not be picketing his theatre and neither would any people from our church. At that point his interest perked up and he asked me to tell him my name again. I affirmed again that, though we would not be attending the play, we would not set out to cause him any problems. He asked the name of our church. As we were concluding our discussions I went a step further. I was aware of his attempts to fund raise for the theatre to keep it running and I told him that we would like to give him a cheque for £500 to help his efforts. He was stunned and thanked me.

An hour later I was contacted by the BBC and asked to make comment from my rather unusual perspective. This gave me an amazing opportunity to speak positively for the Church and the cause of Christ – but to a much larger audience. I share this story to make this point: God speaks through His Church – what is He saying through yours? How are you "showing" Christ to others? Is what you are saying, either with literal words or by your actions, in line with God's heart for the lost, in line with His heart, His desires? This is worth our careful consideration and meditation.

The way people get to know what God is like is through His Church and those who populate it. There is no other way to become a Christian, except by hearing the good news through people you meet. For this reason we need to regularly "audit" the message of our churches. What are we saying? What are our services communicating? What message do people "get" when they visit the church's bathroom?! What "message" do people hear from the car park attendants or welcome team? This applies at every level of church life. What does your website look like or your event graphics? Do they scream "clipart" and "Publisher" or do they look professional? I know this is a well worn issue, but what about the coffee or tea you provide on Sunday? Is it an "el cheapo" brand or have you decided to make drip filter coffee and offer people twelve varieties of tea? To some these will seem like unimportant details. To me they say something more. Details are taken care of by people who care!

In short, does our message communicate life, excellence, care and thoughtfulness or does it speak of dry rituals, aging traditions and mean-spiritedness? If it's the latter, then our "message" will be swiftly confined to the waste paper basket of society. We must not allow ourselves to be viewed as an anachronism, a relic from another time and place. Is anyone else out there reading this book tired of church buildings being tourist attractions instead of soul saving stations?

It has been said that people want the Church to "show us how you care before you tell us what you know". I'm not trying to water down the focus of the salvation message that calls people to repentance and a confession of faith in Christ. But I do believe we need to connect with people first, before we communicate the need for repentance. Look at the example of Jesus and the woman at the well.[76] First of all Jesus initiated a conversation about water! What about the woman caught in adultery?[77] Jesus went to lengths to communicate that He loved her and didn't condemn her before expressing His thoughts on her current situation.

All of this leads me to reiterate: there is nothing more important than the local church. It's Christ's vehicle for speaking and acting. It is not peripheral, but absolutely central to what God is doing right now in our world.

God's intentions fulfilled through the Church

Read the following scriptures with me. Spend time meditating on them and allow your heart and spirit to remain open to what God wants to say to you regarding His favourite subject, the Church. I find these passage inspiring:

> Ephesians 3:10–11 tells us that God's intent is made manifest through the local church.
>
> "His intent was that now, through the church, the manifold wisdom of God should be made known to the rulers and authorities in the heavenly realms according to his eternal purpose which he accomplished in Christ Jesus our Lord."

God has intentions, a purpose, an aim and an objective. He moves with a sense of determination. God is deliberate. He does things on purpose, never by accident. He never starts a project with the words, "I wonder how this will work out?" His plan is to make known His wisdom *through the Church*. We are the agency through which He will reveal to the world the truth about what has been accomplished through His Son, Jesus. The wisdom of God, and therefore the central message of the Church, is that a way back to God has been made. The wall of hostility that once separated man from God has been pulled down through the death and resurrection of Jesus.

Paul declares in Romans 5:8-10 that "God demonstrates his own love for us in this: While we were still sinners, Christ died for us. Since we have now been justified by his blood, how much more shall we be saved from God's wrath through him! For if, when we were God's enemies, we were reconciled to him through the death of his Son, how much more, having been reconciled, shall we be saved through his life!"

Christ died – a perfect sacrifice prepared from before time. His blood was shed as a result of His death and that shed blood now justifies those who put their faith in Him as Lord. God's wrath, anger and judgement of sin were borne by Jesus so we can now be reconciled to God and brought into new relationship with Him.

So vast is the wisdom of God in salvation that it was not fully revealed until now. The plan was so profound, so complete and so intricate that Peter writes these insightful words in 1 Peter 1:10-12:

> "Concerning this salvation, the prophets, who spoke of the grace that was to come to you, searched intently and with the greatest care, trying to find out the time and circumstances to which the Spirit of Christ in them was pointing when he predicted the sufferings of Christ and the glories that would follow. It was revealed to them that they were not serving themselves but you, when they spoke of the things that have now been told you by those who have preached the gospel to you by the Holy Spirit sent from heaven. Even angels long to look into these things."

This awesome message of salvation is being made known through the Church and it was God's intention for it to be made known this way. The Church is the sole agency charged with the responsibility of communicating this momentous message. Conveying this message of salvation through Christ is the Church's utmost priority. This is why we must urgently cooperate with and carry out the Master Architect's plans.

Ephesians 3:10 says that this wisdom is being made known to "… the rulers and authorities in the heavenly realms." This is the fourth occurrence of the phrase "in heavenly realms" in this epistle. Try to picture, if you can, God's multifaceted wisdom concerning redemption being made apparent through the Church. Imagine heavenly beings observing the Church and seeing in it this unfolding wisdom, the transformational power of redemption. It appears from this scripture that both good and evil angels are watching and that they stand amazed, stunned at the working of God in redeemed men and women. How awesome is salvation. How glorious the power of redemption. What a miracle the Church is.

I see a lot of good, worthy agencies in the earth doing good, worthwhile work. Some of these agencies are helping people find Christ. But God's clear and primary intent is that the power of this message will be made known through the Church. God is determined that this should be the case, so we should not try to divert His plans. We need to be clear and keep our priorities straight when it comes to what we put our resources and energy into. What could happen then, if we really believed the truth of this passage? What could we accomplish with Heaven's help? What if God's determination became our determination? What could take place in our lives and ministries if we lived with this truth uppermost in our minds?

The Church is God's chosen way of impacting the world and if we believe this then we will walk in the truth and revelation of it.

Think about this! How does this truth impact you? How will this truth impact your leadership style and the messages you prepare for people every week? How will it impact the church or the team you lead? We need to strategically and firmly align ourselves with God's purposes and respond to His intentions concerning His Church. Too many churches are distracted and sidetracked. On the face of it, these seem like really good distractions too! But they are distractions nonetheless. My commitment and my determination as a leader is to keep the main thing the main thing and not get side tracked. As Paul wrote in 2 Corinthians 5:18-20:

> "All this is from God, who reconciled us to himself through Christ and *gave us the ministry of reconciliation*: that God was reconciling the world to himself in Christ, not counting men's sins against them. And he has committed to us the message of reconciliation. We are therefore Christ's ambassadors, as though God were making his appeal through us."

We are Christ's ambassadors and God is making His appeal to all mankind through us. We have the ministry of reconciliation, connecting the world to God in Christ. The local church is the "embassy" of the kingdom of Heaven on Earth. This is our purpose in Him. God's design is that through the Church the timeless and unchanging message of salvation is to be proclaimed. We are called to present this unchanging message to a fast-paced and ever-changing world.

Notes

76. John chapter 4
77. John 8:3

7

THE IMPACT AND FOCUS OF THE CHURCH

"My success, part of it certainly, is that I have focused in on a few things."
—Bill Gates

"Focusing your life solely on making a buck shows a certain poverty of ambition. It asks too little of yourself; because it's only when you hitch your wagon to something larger than yourself that you realize your true potential."
—Barack Obama

"Leaders establish the vision for the future and set the strategy for getting there; they cause change. They motivate and inspire others to go in the right direction and they, along with everyone else, sacrifice to get there."
—John Kotter
professor at Harvard Business School

> "So there was great joy in that city."
> (Acts 8:8)

The great challenge of the Church is to keep the main thing the main thing. We get so diverted from our priority that we start doing all sorts of things that water down and dilute our presence in the world. Let's remind ourselves of the core mandate that Jesus gave to His people:

"Then Jesus came to them and said, 'All authority in heaven and on earth has been given to me. Therefore go and make disciples of all nations, baptizing them in the name of the Father and of the Son and of the Holy Spirit, and teaching them to obey everything I have commanded you. And surely I am with you always, to the very end of the age.'" (Matthew 28:18)

I want to take some time in this chapter to unpack these verses as they speak of the power and supremacy of Christ, and by implication His Church, in our world. Ask God to speak to you with fresh revelation as we examine this well worn passage of scripture.

1. All authority was given to Jesus and therefore by Jesus to His church. The Church was never to be an insipid, inconsequential group, peripheral to the world, but rather an empowered, cutting edge force with authority and divine purpose. The Church founded by Christ was to be powerful, significant and influential, a living, breathing organisation commissioned by Heaven to act, speak and exert power on Jesus' behalf, to preach salvation, heal the sick and set people free.

The Church is meant to be apostolic with a breakthrough spirit, challenging the powers of darkness, standing against spiritual principalities. We are called to pull down strongholds and experience the impact of the kingdom of God wherever we go. We are called to exercise our authority in such a way as to significantly influence our towns, cities and nations.

2. This authority was given in Heaven and on Earth! God has a plan to establish the greatness of His name in the Earth. The Lord's name is great, but when we think of the greatness of His name we tend to think of Heaven and not Earth.

Mankind, and even Satan, does not mind God ruling the heavens, but desires to keep Him out of the Earth! When Satan could not overthrow God's rule in Heaven he set out to interfere with God's rule on the Earth and destroy His plan in the world. Satan enticed Adam and Eve to rebel against God's rule and ever since man has been trying to establish the greatness of his own name in the Earth. We only need to look at incidents such as the tower of Babel in Genesis 11 to see how desperately man attempts to do this. In the end it's root is in an ungodly pride and arrogance.

Mankind in their spiritual blindness have rejected the visible evidence of the greatness of God and sought to remove His name from society's structures – government, education, medicine and even the family structure. Just take a look at the modern secular structures of the European Union. They have been successful in removing any mention of God from their constitutions.

Man is constantly battling God for the right to "rule". Often we find ourselves fighting not against demonic powers but simply the nature of man! Even believers can say they want to glorify God and yet not submit to His kingdom rule. There is a scenario where some are happy that Jesus is "resident but not president." And yet, the authority of Christ is to reign on the Earth through the Church. We must learn to cooperate with that authority.

3. The Church is to always be outward in its focus. The Church's job is to be "going into the entire world." We are to be always moving forward, spreading out and going into ethnic and societal grouping. The Church must be constantly "on a mission" to take the Gospel far and wide, beginning with our own neighbourhood and to the ends of the Earth. Here we see a picture of an adventurous Church, a pioneering Church, a prevailing Church obedient to the Word of its Builder and Architect. It is a picture of a growing Church, an increasing Church and a relentless Church set upon fulfilling the mission of our Leader before we die. Jesus has mandated the Church to penetrate the darkness of our world, to go into every situation with the life-changing message of salvation.

A static and stationary Church will soon stagnate. A static Church is out of sync with Heaven. There must be *movement* – not an uncoordinated jangling of body parts, but a strategic, focused "going out" into the world to share the greatest message on Earth. As we determine to "go" God is faithful to act and mighty to save.[78] The Church He is building is motivated by a concern to see the lost saved and people added to its number on a regular basis. Any church where people are not being saved is not functioning well and is not healthy. The Church was never meant to be an inward-focused, navel-gazing organisation caught up with its own survival, meeting its own needs and keep "sinners" at arm's length. A quick look at any church's annual budget will reveal its true focus: what percentage of funds are spent on internal programs and what percentage on mission and outward-looking local programmes designed to reach the lost? Yes, people will always have needs and we should minister to those needs. The early Church recognised needs amongst the believers and they ministered to one another,[79] but their primary motivation was always the cause of Christ, to seek out those who had not yet received salvation.[80]

To these first believers it was more important to reach the lost than anything else. As Paul expressed in 2 Corinthians 5:14, "Christ's love compels us, because we are convinced that one died for all, and therefore all died." Again in Acts 4:20, Luke writes, "For we cannot help speaking about what we have seen and heard." This desire was what propelled them forward and prevented them from becoming insular. It would never do just to bless the faithful and teach them the "meat of the word."[81] They simply had to reach lost people; their destiny was defined by this. They were a group who understood the command to "GO." The Church was evangelistic. In Acts 8 we see a great persecution come upon the Church, but rather than deterring them they turned this "scattering" of the Church to their advantage. Their spreading out led them to speak to the Samaritans about Jesus, with great success. From there the ministry of Peter took the Gospel to the Gentiles and Paul brought the message to world through his missionary journeys.

I tend to see it this way: when we become followers of Jesus He takes a few months to make sure we are established in our faith and then God gives us a shove in the right direction. "Go," He says. Our responses to this can be interesting. "But Lord, I want to hang out with you." "No," says Jesus, "it's time for you to go into your world. But don't worry, I'll be with you by my Spirit."

4. *Jesus said "All power is given unto me in heaven and in earth" (Matthew 28:18).* We have no problem believing that God is powerful, but Satan constantly deceives believers into thinking God has "limited" power on the Earth. Yet, Psalm 24:1 tells us explicitly, "The earth is the Lord's and the fullness thereof the world and they that dwell therein."

2 Corinthians 4:4 refers to Satan as the "god" (with a little "g") of this world and its evil systems and the one who influences this world's values and morals. But the Earth is *the Lord's*. This planet belongs to our God. God has a presence on the Earth through His people, the Church. Often we have little expectation of God displaying His strength here on Earth, but this is exactly what He wants us to do!

Act 2 is a record of how Jesus began immediately to release power to the Apostles to use in the Earth to make His name great. Almost straight away the disciples saw thousands of people responding to their preaching and they began to work miracles and cast out demons. These spiritual gifts were then imparted to others, apart from the twelve Apostles. Other "disciples" began to move powerfully under the anointing of the Holy Spirit and God was with them too.[82]

Because the Church is a supernatural organism, created and sustained by Christ, it is perfectly natural that we should exert the same spiritual power as our Leader. Jesus promised this and the promise holds true not just for those early believers, but for all His disciples for all time: "But you will receive power when the Holy Spirit comes on you" (Acts 1:8). This is the power Jesus was speaking about earlier in Luke 24: 49 when He told the disciples to "stay in the city until you have been clothed with power from on high." This is our power to be witnesses and to go into the world and impact people's lives with salvation and healing or by using some other "power gift" from God.

5. *"Make disciples …"* It was 300 years before a church building was constructed to house a church service. Early Christians didn't have the "bricks and mortar" mentality that many are beset by today. Instead they simply understood the command of Jesus to "make disciples". This meant no more than to train and teach people regarding the things Jesus Himself said and did. This clear understanding seems to be clouded for some in the 21st Century Church, yet it is so simple: win people to Christ and then make them into followers of Christ who do the same as He did.

Jesus said we must "make disciples" so the Church must be about building people into the likeness of Christ, both in character and integrity as well the understanding and knowledge of God and His Word. This is part and parcel of what the Church must do – it's not an optional extra – we are to "go" and "make disciples", it's a two-part equation. Jesus' method for this is baptising and teaching. We lead people to Christ, baptise them and then teach them the Word. We baptise and teach while going. We do it all while "on the move" forward.

The promise of Christ is that as we move forward His presence will be with us. We are a Church where Jesus is! Walking close to Jesus is vital and understanding His supremacy is fundamental. He IS with us and we are following Him into the world. He is going before us by the power of His Holy Spirit and preparing the way for us. He has invaded this word, its cultures and languages. He has gone before us.

God has never left a generation bereft of a witness full of His Spirit. If you so desire and are willing to change to be like Him, then there is no reason why your church cannot be an impacting church in this generation.

A Church and a people for each generation

Every generation sees a new Church emerging. I remember during my years in Bible College I had this idea that my denomination was trying to shape me, sort of like a sausage! I know now I was wrong, but the feeling was real at the time. In fact, my perception of my denomination was really the reflection of a desire to simply be "me" but full of God's Spirit, His word and His creativity expressed through my unique personality.

I wasn't interested in being like anyone else in my denomination. That doesn't mean I didn't admire many others, but deep down I knew God had called me, was equipping me and had designs upon my life that would take me where others had not dared to go. I sensed destiny. I knew it was God who put that sense there. I knew God was going to use me and raise me up in my generation to make history. I was really excited about this thought.

Throughout history and in every generation God has raised up men and women to re-emphasise His truth and reality to a dying world. For this reason every church needs to think how it is building its future and recognise the need to reinvent itself from generation to generation. We need to be conscious of leaving a valid legacy to pass on to the next generation. Churches where people grow old and die and, when everyone is dead, they close their doors and shut down are not biblical churches! They are meant to thrive from generation to generation and this means change. What was acceptable for one generation may not be acceptable for the next. If our mission it to reach the lost, then we must do so in a way that is relevant to those around us. The message of the Church is timeless, but our methods of communication must alter from generation to generation.

The truth is, some churches suffer from a self-indulgent spirit and their members attend mostly to have their personal needs met. This is one reason why many churches fail to adapt to the needs of a rising generation. They stick doggedly to a service format some created back in the dark ages, because "that's what people like" or are "comfortable with"! I find it mind boggling that towns and cities are perishing for lack of knowledge while churches slavishly follow their arcane traditions. We have a world to embrace with a life-transforming message. When will we learn that it's not all about us?

I remember early in the transition phase of our church, a dear woman came to me and said, "I think we should sing hymns in church." I had just embarked upon changing the worship style of the church to sing more modern songs from this century and she didn't approve. I tried earnestly to explain why I was doing this and encouraged her to listen to these great hymns at home or in the car. My words fell on deaf ears because she couldn't see beyond her personal preferences and understand that we were in fact trying to reach un-churched people. You can see it coming can't you? I stood my ground and explained myself a few times, but to no avail. I told her this was the future of our church. Within three weeks she told me she felt the Lord was "moving her on". I'm not saying we should never sing hymns either, but every spirit of control must be confronted lovingly and wisely. God seeks to keep His Church up to date and contemporary. One aspect of this is reflected in our choice of songs and worship styles.

It is fraught with many difficulties if you seek to build a "today" church on a "yesterday" platform. Knowing this, God Himself has initiated new moves of His Spirit at various times and in many nations of the Earth. Look at this brief run down:

At the turn of the 16th Century the Catholic Church of the day was riddled with sin, immorality and false doctrine such as the selling of indulgences and the crusades designed to kill Muslims, rape their women and plunder their holy sites. The light of the Gospel was nearly extinguished. It was known as the Dark Ages.

Then a young man named Martin Luther arrived to spearhead a new movement. He championed the forgotten truth of the Word that salvation was by faith alone, justification by faith alone, repentance of sin and confession of Christ was all that was required. He challenged the known religious powers of his day, preached from the Bible, and encouraged people to actually read the Scriptures. This Reformation turned the world upside down.

William Tyndale was the first to print an English New Testament. Tyndale had been forced to flee England because of the widespread rumour that his English New Testament project was underway, causing inquisitors and bounty hunters to hunt him down and try to arrest him to halt the project. But God foiled their plans and in 1525-1526 the Tyndale New Testament became the first printed edition of the Scriptures in the English language.

Over the centuries others came to re-emphasise truths lost to the Church in previous generations:

The Baptist church reemphasised the doctrine and teaching on baptism in water by full emersion.

The Methodist movement founded by John and Charles Wesley preached salvation, taught about church planting, and created contemporary church structures. They caused a great stir wherever they went, drawing huge crowds and preaching with fervour.

The Salvation Army, founded by the Booth family, began as a church to reach the unreachable. They touched the untouchable and changed entire cities with their Gospel message presented through fresh new songs and music. They had to start new churches because the older generation of believers couldn't cope with the kinds of people getting saved and joining the church – prostitutes, alcoholics, thieves and criminals, not to mention the street urchins who flocked to their Sunday Schools and hostels.

The Holiness movements led by various personalities began to teach on living a holy life by the power of the Holy Spirit, leading to a revival of seeing people coming to Christ, declarations of repentance and crowds of people falling down under the presence of the Holy Spirit.

Revivalists with preaching that stirred cities and nations affected nations as thousands accepted Jesus as Lord and Saviour.

The Pentecostals with their emphasis on the Baptism in the Holy Spirit and speaking in tongues launched an earth shattering move of power that encircled the globe as the Church began to see miracles again! It was awe inspiring as healing crusades took place and women like Kathryn Kuhlman and Aimee Semple McPherson astounded crowds across the globe. Men like Smith Wigglesworth and the Jeffery brothers brought the truth of divine healing back to the Church.

The Charismatic movement brought renewal for so many churches, both Pentecostal and mainstream. During this time many were horrified that God began to pour out the Holy Spirit upon Catholics and other mainline traditional churches!

New teaching in this last century flooded the Church with new insights into,

The baptism with the Holy Spirit
The gifts of the Spirit

Casting out demons
The need for exposition in preaching
Praise and worship, with hours of singing in the Spirit worshipping God
Becoming a contemporary church with an up-to-date message
The introduction of other musical instruments into praise and worship, like guitars and drums, previously thought to be the devil's tools, leading to new musical styles

Imagine the horror as good Christians saw their churches filled with lights, smoke machines and industrial style sound systems. Back in the late 60s and early 70s men like Chuck Smith and churches like Calvary Chapel off Newport Beach introduced the Jesus movement. 10,000 young University students arrived at church dressed like flower children in jeans, with bare feet and tie-dyed clothing. Long haired hippies were becoming Christians! But how interesting that a similar cycle had taken place over a hundred years previously with the Salvation Army as William Booth wrote Christian lyrics to the popular pub tunes of his day. Remember that the Wesleys were thrown out of mainstream churches because their music was not "worshipful" and their style of preaching unorthodox. Plus, their method of church planting was unconventional and untraditional! They suffered the same criticism as many contemporary churches!

Yet, God has always been faithful to establish His presence in every generation and place. From before the foundations of the Earth God had a plan for redeeming mankind from the folly and foolishness of sin. His plan was accomplished in the incarnation of His Son, the Lord Jesus Christ. As The Message translation of John 1:14 says, "The Word became flesh and blood, and moved into the neighbourhood."

As the Church we need to get real, be authentic, and become touchable and user-friendly for our generation. We need to be a "today" church with a "tomorrow" platform; contemporary yet prophetic. I am not talking simply about cutting edge technology or slick bands with cool music, but rather about a spirit that says, "We want to be real, genuine and true to God and who He created us to be." God has equipped us to do it. As the writer of Hebrews puts it:

> "May the God of peace, who through the blood of the eternal covenant brought back from the dead our Lord Jesus, that great Shepherd of the sheep, equip you with everything good for doing his will, and may he work in us what is pleasing to him, through Jesus Christ, to whom be glory forever and ever. Amen." (Hebrews 13:20-21)

Notes

78. Zephaniah 3:17
79. Acts 2:45, Acts 4:35, Acts 6:1
80. Romans 15:20, 2 Corinthians 10:14-16
81. Hebrews 5:12-14
82. E.G. Stephen in Acts 6:8

Part Two

A RENAISSANCE OF KEY VALUES

8

WHO'S BUILDING WHOSE CHURCH?

"God is in the details."
—Ludwig Mies van der Rohe,
German born American architect 1886 – 1969

"And I tell you that you are Peter, and on this rock I will build
my church,
and the gates of Hades will not overcome it."
(Matthew 16:18)

The most fundamental question a church leader can ask is this: "Who is building whose church?" There are only four possible answers and therefore four scenarios we might encounter:

1. Jesus is building MY church
2. I'M building Jesus' church

3. I'M building MY Church
4. Jesus is building HIS Church

Surprising as it may sound, all four scenarios are alive and well in the world today, so let's take a look at the defining characteristics of each situation.

1. Jesus is building MY church

In this kind of church leaders and church members have cultivated a culture where they recognise God's love but not His authority. Their unspoken mentality is, "God is love … but don't tell me what to do."

The church under construction then becomes MY church, MY spiritual home. The priority is that this church should meet MY needs and the needs of MY family. Anything that unsettles this desire is seen a threat, even when the threat is God Himself seeking to intervene to bring direction or correction.

The New Testament example of this is found in Revelation 3:1–8 in the words of Jesus to the church at Sardis: "You have a name of being alive but you are dead!"

This is a church that is introverted. It is not outward looking because people believe Jesus is building a church "for them". If that is so, then the lost millions are less important. Who cares so long as they have MY favourite preacher, play MY favourite songs and the volume of the band doesn't hurt MY ears. Then I'm happy, because this is MY church.

This church talks a lot about salvation, but usually in terms of MY salvation. It focuses on MY testimony and experiences. Spiritual gifts are also introverted, making them primarily a blessing for ME, to fulfil MY destiny, MY purpose and MY call.

There are lots of ministries in these kinds of churches but with a subtle shift – they are all ministering to the local body. The number of programmes with an outward focus are few and watered down. A large percentage of the church's finance is spent on them. Little is used to evangelize the lost. The programmes are ME centred. The women's group is for ME, the youth group and Sunday school is for MY children, and the list goes on.

The leadership of this kind of church has a priority to please people above pleasing God. This kind of leader responds to the gripes and groans of church members more than the Holy Spirit's direction, revelation and instruction!

The leaders of this kind of church are fire fighters rather than fire starters.

This kind of church has a style that is comfortable for a certain type of person, regardless of age or convention. It is a church where I feel at home because it is MY church Jesus is building.

This is church ruled by people's personal preferences. This kind of church is an expert at politics and subversion. Its people reject anything that will upset the status quo and will do all in their power to stop it. With this scenario being played out the church becomes a means to an end and operates predictably to simply meet MY needs.

It is possible for even a "modern church" to fall prey to this error. They work hard to build a church that meets people's needs, but in the long run people will gravitate towards the "Bono phenomenon" and sing, "I still haven't found what I'm looking for." Why? Because this model is not what the Master is building and so ultimately unfulfilling.

2. I'M building Jesus' church

These sorts of churches operate at a high pace. They are busy churches. But their busyness has a subtle edge to it – it is a group of people *working hard* to build Jesus' church, but taking the initiative out of His hands.

The New Testament example is the Ephesian Church that Jesus speaks to in Revelation Chapter 2:1–7: "These are the words of him who holds the seven stars in his right hand and walks among the seven golden lamp stands: I know your deeds, your hard work and your perseverance. I know that you cannot tolerate wicked men, that you have tested those who claim to be apostles but are not, and have found them false. You have persevered and have endured hardships for my name, and have not grown weary. Yet I hold this against you: You have forsaken your first love" (NIV).

This sort of church grows a people-orientated culture. It applauds people who labour tirelessly for God. It knows how to honour people and is a thankful church. This sort of church has a well-developed "volunteer culture" because their philosophy is that *we are building* His church.

This kind of church develops a people who feel it is their job to "present" God with a trophy or prize that we have created. But the emphasis is again on us: OUR service, OUR ministries, OUR work. It's philosophy is, "Lord, I'm working hard for you. I'm out every night of the week doing things for Jesus."

This kind of church tends to be removed from the world. As Christine Caine says, "They are neither in the world nor part of it!"

Some churches like this develop a culture of legalism; a system of rules to keep people in line.

They are extremely hectic churches because they have taken their emphasis off the Lord and transferred it onto meetings, attendance and performance. This kind of church is event-orientated, but tends to focus more on the events themselves than the reason for running them.

This kind of church works *for* Jesus not *with* Him. They are so busy working for Jesus that they forget to spend time with Him.

This is a church whose default leadership model is to be "highly spiritual" shrouding biblical truth and making it seem inaccessible to ordinary mortals, which reinforces the leaders' position of influence and power. But Jesus rebukes this kind of church. It has lost sight of its first love and needs to repent and return to Him.

3. I'M building MY church

At first glance it sounds nonsensical, but there is such a thing as a "secular" church! It looks like a church, sings like a church, prays like a church and even talks like a church, but it is building a culture that acknowledges God is there, but doesn't allow Him the opportunity to do anything in the church because THEY are building THEIR church!

The New Testament example of this is found in the words of Jesus to the church at Laodicea recorded in Revelation 3:15-18: "I know your deeds, that you are neither cold nor hot. I wish you were either one or the other! So, because you are lukewarm – neither hot nor cold – I am about to spit you out of my mouth. You say, 'I am rich; I have acquired wealth and do not need a thing.' But you do not realise that you are wretched, pitiful, poor, blind and naked" (NIV).

This church's culture is centred on humanistic philosophies, Christianized principles for success that are devoid of faith. This church constantly plays it safe. They are supremely cautious in what they do and don't risk doing anything that might upset their formula for success.

This church has a controlling culture that seeks to direct people rather than release them into fruitful ministry. This church is very conscious of titles and positions. They thrive on the power such positions give them.

This kind of church is building-conscious and creates a culture where the building is as important if not more important than the actual people. They say things like, "Don't move the communion table! … Don't touch the banners! … You can't move those chairs, don't you know they've been there for 10,000 years!"

It's not just older or more traditional denominational churches that fall into this category, modern independent churches can fall prey to it too.

This church has developed a culture that acknowledges God but does not desire His intervention in the administration of the church. Prayer is for "things", for needs, and to ask God to bless, but not for direction or insight because, "We know what the Lord wants."

Some of these churches have people who "look" sort of like Christians and "act" like ministers, but whose hearts are politically motivated, traditional, and structure conscious. 2 Timothy 3:4-5 describes them well, having "a form of godliness but denying its power." Paul's advice is, "Have nothing to do with them."

This church has a culture that does not savour the things of God. They are not interested in true biblical leadership, the anointing of God, faith or the moving of the Holy Spirit.

Because this group does not take pleasure in the things of God, God says He will literally, "vomit them from His mouth"!

4. Jesus is building HIS church

We all know what Jesus said though. He said, "HE will build HIS church."

This kind of church intentionally builds a culture that seeks God and asks Him, "What are Your ideas? What do You want to do in Your church?" This church wants to be found doing what He is doing.

This kind of church has a leader who resists the desire to become a superstar and is constantly directing people back to Jesus Christ, the One and only Superstar for all times.

This kind of church intentionally seeks to produce servant-hearted men and women. They are not overly conscious of titles, are not enamoured by positions, and their simple delight is to be found doing whatever it requires to build the church.

Leaders in these kinds of churches know how to graciously step aside when another comes along to lead who can do it better than them. They realise that what got them to "here" is not going to take them to the next level, and so are happy when others "rise up" around them.

This church develops a culture that is passionate about God, in love with Jesus and radically open to the Holy Spirit. This kind of church really loves God and is excited about knowing Him. Its members ask each other, "What is God saying to you?" They are relational with God and prayer is a two-way street.

This church has a culture that is hungry for the Word of God. The Word is their daily recharge. They seek God's will. They desire to know His mind as they diligently search the Scriptures to discover His plan for their lives.

This church develops a culture of knowing God, seeking Him and waiting on Him to hear from His Word and do His will. Jesus is building *His church* so its people willingly submit to His will with humility.

This kind of church loves people of all ages, race and religious background. They love people because God Himself loved people so much that He gave His Son Jesus to die for them.

This kind of Church is incredibly generous of heart. People are more than numbers, they are valuable to God and to those who lead the church. People are honoured and their dignity is respected. Relationships are encouraged to blossom because the leaders know that as Jesus builds His church every ministry flows out of good relationships, unity and an attitude of love and respect. Friendships are important and marriages are sacred.

When Jesus is building His Church people acknowledge, honour and work with the "gift ministry" Jesus has placed within the church. This church's culture recognises and respects the gift of God in men and women of God

Whilst honouring the gifts of men and women, this church

helps build others to do the work of the ministry. There is no clergy, no laity, and everyone is a minister. There are no spectators because everyone is involved and serving in the house.

This church looks at the world and sees life through the eyes of the Saviour whose great mission is to seek and save those who are lost. They see sinners before they see sin, people before sexual orientations, human beings before titles, positions or status.

This is a church that makes little or no comment on age groups because it is a place where young and old meet together with a common purpose in God. Though there are age-relevant programmes, the church is primarily a family, a body and building of God's design.

If Jesus is building His church then, as He leads, its people commence ministries that touch a needy world. This church is truly motivated by the cause of Christ to seek and save.

This church understands the need for discipleship and makes followers of Christ to increase the workforce for reaching a needy world.

If Jesus is building His church then the emphasis is all on HIM, not US! We are involved at every level because we are His people, His body, but He is always the centre. We are simply His hands and His feet ready to touch a needy world.

When Jesus is free to build His church, people are developed to be servants of His house. They sense destiny and believe they are called for such a time as this, to bring deliverance to a city, a nation and beyond.

When it is Jesus building His church the people become those who simply flow with Him and His appointed gift-people to see His vision fulfilled in the earth. They work hard, but do not strive in their own strength.

When Jesus is building His church, people are characterized by a spirit of generosity in all areas. They give unstintingly to the cause of Christ. They support every good work with either their finance or their physical energy. It is a church that loves people and uses money, not loves money and uses people!

When Jesus is doing the building then the people will always seek to reflect His glory in their lives. His excellence and majesty is translated into the way the church functions. The church's plans and work display the colours of Heaven.

When Jesus is building His church He leads His people into mission. This is a church that reaches out to people, that is burdened by the lost, that weeps for those who don't know the power of Christ, that is vexed by unrighteousness and knows the only answer is a saving knowledge of Christ. This passion is the motivation of their hearts because it is the motivation of His heart.

Jesus is longing to build a Church that looks like this and desires to work with us to do it! Our role is one of humble servants who desire to do His will. We need to pray with Bob Pierce, the founder of World Vision, "May my heart be moved by what moves the heart of God." Together, we have been given the amazing opportunity and privilege to make a difference in our world as we demonstrate lives that point to our generous Father. We are to be salt and light:

"Let me tell you why you are here. You're here to be salt-seasoning that brings out the God-flavours of this earth. If you lose your saltiness, how will people taste godliness? You've lost your usefulness and will end up in the garbage. Here's another way to put it: You're here to be light, bringing out the God-colours in the world. God is not a secret to be kept. We're going public with this, as public as a city on a hill. If I make you light-bearers, you don't think I'm going to hide you under a bucket, do you? I'm putting you on a light stand. Now that I've put you there on a hilltop, on a light stand—shine! Keep open house; be generous with your lives. By opening up to others, you'll prompt people to open up with God, this generous Father in heaven."

The Church – the agency of Heaven

As the people of God, the Church, we have a responsibility: a mandate to establish His will and kingdom here on Earth. We are called to co-labourers with Him and to build His House in such a way that people everywhere are given a glimpse of Heaven. Paul captures this fantastic concept in vivid colour in his writings.

> "And God placed all things under his feet and appointed him to be head over everything for the church, which is his body, the fullness of him who fills everything in every way." (Ephesians 1:22-23)

And again in Ephesians 1:23-25:

> "All this energy issues from Christ: God raised him from death and set him on a throne in deep heaven, in charge of running the universe, everything from galaxies to governments, no name and no power exempt from his rule. And not just for the time being, but forever. He is in charge of it all, has the final word on everything. At the centre of all this, Christ rules the church, the church, you see, is not peripheral to the world; the world is peripheral to the church. The church is Christ's body, in which he speaks and acts, by which he fills everything with his presence." (The Message)

And in Ephesians: 3:9-11:

> "His intent was that now, through the church, the manifold wisdom of God should be made known to the rulers and authorities in the heavenly realms, according to his eternal purpose which he accomplished in Christ Jesus our Lord."

We clearly see God's intentions! We see that through the local church His wisdom and power is to be made known to rulers and authorities in accordance with the eternal purpose accomplished through Jesus Christ in His death and resurrection.

Bill Hybels said, "The local Church is the hope of the world and the future lies in the hands of its leaders." This, if you dare to believe it, is life transforming and city shaking!

Paul also wrote in Ephesians: 3:20, "Now to him who is able to do immeasurably more than all we ask or imagine, according to his power that is at work within us, to him be glory in the church and in Christ Jesus throughout all generations, forever and ever! Amen."

What do you believe about the church you lead? Could your church ever touch the world? Is it possible that it could impact your city or town? Could you begin to see hundreds coming to Christ each year, month or week? Could it happen for you?

As I read this scripture, and somebody tell me if I'm taking it out of context, it says that God is able to do "immeasurably MORE than all we ask or imagine." This sounds glorious – glorious for the Church and bringing glory to Jesus. All we're asking for and imagining about His church can happen according to His power – the same power that raised Jesus from the dead; the same power that saves a life; the same power that energised the early Church. This is the same power that now works with us. We need to be inspired and stretched to believe for more for the churches we lead!

The church is the agency of God in the Earth today to declare His glory and proclaim His mercy, salvation and forgiveness. The Church exists to bring glory to God. It exists to reflect the atmosphere, energy, life, health and goodness of the House of God in Heaven. We are called as God's people to bring Heaven to the House[83] and allow the Church to be the glorious place she is meant to be. Our local church can echo Heaven. Our church is called to reflect the life, sound, peace and the presence of the place where God Himself dwells.

When God responded to the needs of fallen mankind, incarnation was the plan He chose – sending Jesus into our world with a covering of flesh and blood. As The Message puts it, "God moved into the neighbourhood". This is awesome news! As Jesus is free to build His Church His way, He presences Himself in the midst of us and Heaven comes down to Earth[84]. And Heaven is characterised by His goodness, grace, blessing, abundance, joy, excellence, magnificence, power and fullness. All of this fills us, touches us and empowers us.

I find this thought irresistible and I believe the house of God should be irresistible to others, with a magnetic pull. Let me ask a few challenging questions: is your Christianity irresistible? Is your church culture irresistible to the people in your community? Are people drawn to you because there is "life" in the church? Does your church have the "wow" factor? Do you exemplify a lifestyle of devotion and excellence?

We can have all this and more but we need to allow Jesus to build His Church and to infuse His people with these values. His House can and will be a place of power, overflow, abundance and peace – but we must cooperate with the Master Builder.

An open heaven

The Church is a group of people who can experience God's abundance under an open Heaven. I believe this is what God desires for us: a House so awesome that the gates of Hell will not be able to overcome it; a House the world will look at in utter amazement over. This could be your local church.

There is no one with a greater desire to build His Church than Jesus Himself. He loves the church and wants to see it touch cities, nations and the world. As Jesus builds His Church He wants Heaven in His House. He desires to have a Church that people call "home," where people come in and instantly know they have arrived in a safe place. We will only see this when we abandon all other models of build church except allowing Jesus to build *His Church, His way*.

Notes

83. *Heaven is in This House*, Bobbie Houston, Maximised Leadership Inc., 2001.
84. Zephaniah 3:17

9

THE HOUSE OF GOD – RESTORING KEY VALUES

"I have chosen and consecrated this temple so that my Name
may be there forever.
My eyes and my heart will always be there."
(2 Chronicles 7:16)

"Almost any man worthy of his salt would fight to defend his
home, but no one ever heard of a man going to war for his
boarding house"
—Mark Twain

In order to align ourselves with God's plans for His Church and to immerse ourselves in helping Jesus to build His Church, His way, I believe we need to restore certain key values to the heart of our churches. In this chapter we will focus on what I believe are three pivotal values: 1. That we live with an awareness that God has chosen and sanctified His House to fulfil His purposes, 2. That we restore among our ranks a sense of awe in God's House, and 3. That we recognise the expansive energy God has invested in His Church and live to release it! Let's look at each of these in turn:

Key value 1: God has chosen and sanctified His house

The Message translation of 2 Chronicles 7:16 says, "Believe me, I've chosen and sanctified this Temple that you have built: My Name is stamped on it forever; my eyes are on it and my heart in it always."

When God says He's *chosen* something it is imperative that we know what it is He has chosen. When God *sanctifies* or separates something we should know and understand what it is He has taken the time to separate and make holy. Why? Because what He sanctifies is anointed, empowered, and a place where His glory resides!

It is His *House* that has garnered this kind of attention. The Church is the object of God's holy attention. Why then do we denigrate what God has chosen and sanctified, first of all by allowing it to be sidetracked by peripheral issues, and also by approaching it with such a consumerist mentality?

For years I have seen leaders get sidetracked from focusing on the House of God. They get involved in all sorts of "good activities": schools, charities, youth work, radio stations, street pastors and other ecumenical activities – none of which are wrong in and of themselves, *unless* they are allowed to become a distraction from our primary mission and priority focus.

The world around us has relegated the church to irrelevance and almost forgotten about us because of the way much of the Church treats the Church! In many places God's people are to be found building something other than that which He has decreed.

We have lost our way and become sidetracked with our own people and programmes. Outsiders look at church life and see things they should never see in the body of Christ: believers arguing over the colour of the carpet and which songs to sing, who gets to lead various ministries. Politics and sedition are more apparent in some local churches than prayer and seeking God's presence. Ouch!

Believe me, when you embark upon a transition to transform your local church into an entity that displays beauty and truth, get ready for some resistance. The devil hates this kind of church and the carnal nature of man also resists it with a vengeance! But don't worry too much, because conflict is revealing and God is on your side.

My name is stamped on it FOREVER!

Even more significant than the fact that God has chosen and sanctified His House is the thought in this verse that He has "stamped" His name upon it. In other words, the Church has the imprint of deity all over it. The plan concerning the House of God, devised before the foundation of the world, conceived in Heaven, imagined by the Trinity, visualised by Jesus and created by the Holy Spirit, has been copyrighted by the Father and personally branded by Him!

Deep in the recesses of the universe, in the heart of the triune God, the concept of CHURCH was created and signed off. This is God's idea completely! How appropriate then is it for us to pause regularly and ask, "Are we working according to His divine plan? Are we building this with You and Your guidance God?"

By stamping His name upon it God says of the Church, "This is mine!" God has engraved His name upon His House. It speaks of His ownership, His possession, His commitment to safekeeping. It's like God has created a contract and written His name on it. His name is inerasable – He is contractually bound to the venture of establishing His great Church. He is committed to its success because it is His name on the line. Be careful then how you build. Make sure you are working from the same plans as God.

His eyes are on it

The 2 Chronicles verse tells us that God's eyes are constantly on His House. He is ever watching over it, fully aware of His commitment and responsibilities. This scripture speaks of God's integrity and care in resourcing His House – He is paying attention that it has everything it needs to thrive. He is the Heavenly Watcher. Nothing escapes His attention. No detail is too small for Him to not be interested.

As leaders it pays to wait before God and ask Him what He sees. God's perspectives are eternal and for us His comments are prophetic. Let's regularly ask, "What do you see Lord?" He can warn us of impending attacks and prepare us for the battle. He can show us many things concerning the people we want to work with. Because His eye is ever upon His Church we can ask Him to give us insight into situations and circumstances in the life of the church and we can receive His wisdom and discernment.

His heart is in it always

Finally we read that God's heart is in and for His House, always. His commitment to us as His Church is *heart and soul*, unwavering, absolute and complete. His mind is always engaged in His House's forward movement. God is strategic and creative concerning His House. When His heart is in something then you can be assured that His Spirit is active. Jesus is working to build His House in every corner of the planet.

God is filled with kindness, tenderness and affection towards His Church. Because His *heart* is in it, the House He is building is a House of grace, mercy and abounding love. Because God's *heart* is in this venture, it underlines to us how dynamic and vital it is for us to be moved by His heart! When we touch God's heart, when are moved by what moves Him, we will find ourselves firmly rooted in the centre of His will. If we walk like this, we cannot fail to have our perspective of the Church define us and direct our faith.

Key value 2: Restoring a sense of awe for the house of God

Genesis 28:16-19 relates the experience of Jacob after he has a "dream" in which he encounters God:

> "When Jacob awoke from his sleep, he thought, 'Surely the LORD is in this place, and I was not aware of it.' He was afraid and said, *'How awesome is this place!* This is none other than the house of God; this is the gate of heaven.' Early the next morning Jacob took the stone he had placed under his head and set it up as a pillar and poured oil on top of it. He called that place Bethel, though the city used to be called Luz."

Our contemporary expression of the house of God – the Church – is meant to be an awesome place! Some reading this will struggle with that concept, thinking, my church could not be described as awesome, but hang in there – some changes to the way we think can have incredible impact.

I love the Message version of verses 16-17: "Jacob woke up from his sleep. He said, 'God is in this place—truly. And I didn't even know it!' He was terrified. He whispered in awe, 'Incredible. Wonderful. Holy. This is God's House. This is the Gate of Heaven.'"

Listen to these words whispered in holy terror. Do they describe how you feel about your church? When people come into your expression of the house of God do they whisper in holy awe, "Incredible, wonderful, holy …"? What about those who don't know Christ yet. Do they have a "wow" experience as they arrive at your church? Or do we once again meet their expectations of church as dry, dusty and boring?

This passage says that God's house is not like that. This is the first time in Scripture that the term "God's House" is used. Look at the adjectives used to describe it. Jacob was afraid, filled with a holy reverence. Such is the nature of the Church. It's *awesome!*

I believe that such awe and reverence is what is missing from what many are building. We need to adjust our thinking. Our church is not simply a collection of like-minded people trying to fellowship together without throttling each other – it is a sovereign work of God! It is an awesome and fearful thing that we should not treat lightly. Jacob shuddered in holy fear and so should we. This is what so many are missing: *an awesome reverence for God's House.*

When people forget about the transcendent nature of the Church they allow it, by their carelessness, to descend into boredom and irrelevance. But look and listen – meditate on this: the Church is the "gateway to Heaven"! It is the single agency on Earth that can span the distance from Heaven to Earth. It is a house of salvation where lost people can find their way home and have a relationship with God through His Son, Jesus Christ. It is the place where God's power connects with Earth. It is the place where the miraculous happens and lives are healed and transformed. This is what makes it so awesome!

The context of these verses is that Jacob has made a mess of his life to date by trying to achieve his destiny on his own terms. He falls asleep in the wilderness with only a stone for a pillow – a picture of how low he has brought himself. Yet, God in His grace visits Jacob in a vision and shows him the expansiveness of the future he has for him. Jacob has tried to manufacture his destiny by stealing and deceiving others, but God says He will give him another chance and shows him what his destiny could look like if he cooperates.

When Jacob wakes up, he describes his experience with the words, "this is none other than the house of God." The house of God has become a house of destiny for Jacob and I believe that today, the house of God, His Church, is our house of destiny. As we approach it with the same sense of awe and reverence God will connect us with an expansive future that fulfils all we are meant to be in Him, and fulfils His greater plans for His Church and the salvation of the lost. The Church is our personal house of "dreams and visions", where we step out of our past, like Jacob, and into the destiny God has ordained for us. As we step out of our life and into His life, we are suddenly a vital part of something much bigger than ourselves. Like Jacob, regardless of our former failings, in God's house we are on track to achieve things we never imagined possible.

I have spoken to many leaders who had at one time had a sense of destiny. Some have lost their sense of awe and have placed their dreams on the back burner. But God desires to speak to us and reignite our passion with a fresh revelation of His will and plan for us. We need to position ourselves to receive His revelation, but God doesn't expect us to do spiritual gymnastics – after all, he could speak to Jacob while he was sleeping in the middle of nowhere with his head on a stone! Be open and ask God to re-envision you. He can make your dreams live again and revive your destiny.

Key value 3: The house of God – releasing a new sense of energy!

Matthew 16:17-18 in the Message says,

> "Jesus came back, 'God bless you, Simon, son of Jonah! You didn't get that answer out of books or from teachers. My Father in heaven, God himself, let you in on this secret of who I really am. And now I'm going to tell you who you are, really are. You are Peter, a rock. This is the rock on which I

will put together my church, *a church so expansive with energy that not even the gates of hell will be able to keep it out.'"*

This is a key scripture. Other Bible versions talk about the Church as a relentless and unstoppable force, so full of energy that nothing can stop its forward movement. We see a Church that is expansive, unrestrained and constantly growing.

As leaders, what can we do to cooperate with God so that the Church is expressed as the unstoppable, relentless force it is intended to be, at the centre of the world stage? How do we release this "expansive energy" that Jesus speaks of?

The answer is Christ Himself. How do we release a new sense of energy within our church? By ensuring that Jesus is placed at the very centre of everything we do; by making Him the sole focus of our attention, worship and adoration.

Think about this. It sounds simple, even simplistic, yet it's profound. Let the Holy Spirit speak to you about what it means to return Jesus to centre stage in our churches.

The early Church had a momentum based on the person of Christ and His accomplishments on the cross. The believers were filled with the expectation and anticipation of Christ working through them. As a result the Church was constantly moving forward and growing. They expected and they saw Jesus continuing to work in their midst.

There is a certain ferocity to the forward movement of God's kingdom that is breathtaking. The movement of the Holy Spirit infuses the Church with energy and power causing it to move forward relentlessly. Read again the words of Jesus:

> "From the days of John the Baptist until now, the kingdom of heaven has been forcefully advancing, and forceful men lay hold of it." (Matthew 11:12)

I love this passage. I see a "violent", forceful, determined spirit rising up within leaders who strongly desire to see God's kingdom advancing. Those who "catch" this sense of the Spirit's momentum flow with Him and become an irresistible force. This is what shapes and defines the new breed of church. This forceful Church is a prevailing Church that can break down strongholds that previously have seemed unassailable.

I hear stories from pastors in different parts of the world and some of them tell me that it's hard for the church to grow where they are. Some describe how tough the soil is, seeking to describe the spiritual climate. But I believe if they grasped how much God desires to inject His Church with energy and power, things would begin to look different. The Church is the most valuable entity in His universe and He desires it to make its impact everywhere, regardless of the spiritual climate. We need to realign our thinking with God's Word, because we will never see beyond that which we presently believe. Instead of talking about the difficulties and the hardness of the soil, I prefer to say that my city is under an open heaven, that it is filled with spiritually hungry people with a desire to connect with God. I believe this with all my heart and we are seeing a steady stream of people coming to Christ.

I love the way the Church is portrayed in Scripture as being on the offensive. She moves ever forward and not even the gates of hell can withstand her assault. We are not a Church who is hiding behind Jesus! We are not hanging on for grim life until He comes back! Hell is on the defensive! Scripture does not portray the powers of Hell as being on the attack; it's the Church that is on the attack. I think that's a very different view to the one currently held by many churches. We often teach that the devil is on the attack, but Jesus says the complete opposite! So the Church is not all about holding onto what we've got, it's about retaking ground from the enemy.

As Ephesians 1:20 in The Message says, "All this energy issues from Christ." The energy, force and authority of the Church flows out of the supremacy of Christ.

Notice the verse preceding the one we have focused on here. Jesus tells Peter, "My Father in heaven, God himself, let you in on this secret of who I really am. And now I'm going to tell you who you are, really are." Then Jesus spells out Peter's destiny. This underlines the amazing discovery we have been talking about: that as we grasp who Christ really is, He shows us who we really are!

Why is it so few churches really experience breakthrough? Why are we so ineffective at times? Why aren't more churches growing? I believe it's because so many people don't know who they really are. Many suffer from a lack of confidence and self-esteem issues. We need a fresh revelation of who Jesus is for us, and who we are in Him!

Jesus is great at helping people just like Peter to realise who they are and join in with building His Church – we just need to cooperate with Him.

10

FINDING MEANING AND FUNCTION

Meaning: "What something is intended to be, or actually is, expressed or indicated; the end, purpose, or significance of something."
—Dictionary.com

Function: "The action for which a person or thing is particularly fitted or employed."
—Dictionary.com

Function: "Literally a 'mode of acting.'" Greek word is praxis (prax'-is); practice, i.e. (concretely) an act; by extension, a function: deed, office, or work.
—Strong's concordance

"A corporation is organized as a system – it has this department, that department, that department ... they don't have any

meaning separately; they only can function together. And also the body is a system. Society is a system in some sense. And so on." ?
—David Joseph Bohm
U.S. born British quantum physicist

The verses of Romans 12:4-6 give us an important insight into how the Church and its members should function:

> "Just as each of us has one body with many members, and these members do not all have the same function, so in Christ we who are many form one body, and each member belongs to all the others. We have different gifts, according to the grace given us."

Paul writes of the unity of the "one" body. This body comprises many members and they do not all have the same function. Look at this bullet point summary of Paul's words as he goes on to explain …

> We have different gifts, according to the grace given us
> If a man's gift is prophesying, let him use it in proportion to his faith
> If it is serving, let him serve
> if it is teaching, let him teach
> if it is encouraging, let him encourage
> if it is contributing to the needs of others, let him give generously
> if it is leadership, let him govern diligently
> if it is showing mercy, let him do it cheerfully

All of these gifts and abilities represent different functions of the body. There are those whose function is to speak with insight; those whose role is to serve or teach or encourage others. In addition there are those who meet the needs of others (and Paul encourages them to do so generously), those who can provide leadership and others who are able to show mercy. I'm sure this list could go on and on, and Paul didn't intend it to be comprehensive. Any church leader knows that there is an endless amount of work to be done to ensure the body functions healthily.

The Message translates this passage like this: "In this way we are like the various parts of a human body. Each part gets its meaning from the body as a whole, not the other way around. The body we're talking about is Christ's body of chosen people. Each of us finds our meaning and function as a part of his body. But as a chopped-off finger or cut-off toe we wouldn't amount to much, would we? So since we find ourselves fashioned into all these excellently formed and marvellously functioning parts in Christ's body let's just go ahead and be what we were made to be." (Romans 12:4-5)

The Message has an interesting turn of phrase. Every person wants to find their meaning and place in the world. Here we read that it is only as we engage as a part of Christ's body, the Church, that we find our place. It is the Church that gives each person their sense of meaning and function, the Church that equips us with a sense of purpose and destiny.

If in the Church we "find our meaning and function as part of the body" then it is vital that we become a participant in the Church and not merely a spectator or an attendee. Scripture uses vivid picture illustrations for this like being planted like a tree[85] and being built together like living stones.[86] Fundamental to our involvement in Christ's body is the concept that it releases our true purpose and an understanding of how and where we are meant to function.

Becoming a Christian is not just about receiving salvation and a "get out of Hell" card. Inextricably linked to our salvation is our membership in the Church. I'm not talking about registering your details on the church database, but our membership of the body of Christ.

1 Corinthians 12:12-14 says, "The body is a unit, though it is made up of many parts; and though all its parts are many, they form one body. So it is with Christ. For we were all baptised by one Spirit into one body—whether Jews or Greeks, slave or free—and we were all given the one Spirit to drink. Now the body is not made up of one part but of many."

The body of Christ is the Church and we are members of this body, baptised by one Spirit into Christ.[87] It is as we become members of this body at salvation that we begin to receive some revelation about our function within it. This understanding is not transitory, but unfolds over time. This is why it grieves me so to see people join the Church and then leave it. If our purpose and meaning unfolds over time as our relationship with Christ deepens, then some people are tragically cutting short the full extent of their purpose in Him by removing themselves from the Church. No one can say, "I went to church once, found my purpose and then never went back." Our purpose deepens and becomes clearer as we commit ourselves as ongoing participants in the Church. Scripture speaks of us being integrally and essentially connected to God, His mission and His people as part of the Church. This includes its public and corporate gatherings.

I teach that our destiny is attached to the house of God. I teach that as we get into right relationship with Christ and in correct relationship with leadership in His church, we begin to understand our meaning and function. From this point of revelation we can be launched into our destiny. The nature of the Church is that it defines and shapes our future.

I have a young couple in my church who are considering a move to an overseas location. They have been looking at this move for a number of years now. When they first began to consider it they were not in an exciting church situation and so the move looked very appealing. But since connecting with our church they have been faced with a quandary. At last they have found a church that is defining their destiny. They find themselves vitally connected with Christ and His church, are discovering meaning, and have started to function in a biblical context. The desire to move overseas is starting to look less appealing because they have discovered they have a function in the local church. This is what "church" is supposed to achieve.

Body parts

The verse in Romans 12 from The Message also talks about not being a "cut-off toe" i.e. a dismembered body part. I look around the Church scene today and note that there are a lot of "cut-off-toe" people out there. They represent a new demographic of Christians: the ones who don't go to church any more. This group is populated by the disillusioned, the disenchanted and the disappointed. These are Christians who got hurt, offended or just burned out. They say that they believe in God, but not in "church". Others put down their lack of attendance to a hectic and demanding lifestyle.

Whatever the reason, I think this is tragic. In my view, if you are a "cut-off toe" person, *you are a body part, but not a part of the body*. And the implication of not being a part of the body is staggering. It means that, in fact, Christ is not your head. Christianity is a relationship not a religion. Jesus says He is the head of His church, and if you are not connected to that body then, is He really the Lord of your life? Can it be true to say, "I am a Christian but I don't go to church"?

I know! I hear the protests coming thick and fast. Many would call me harsh for making such a statement, but I believe it to be true. People will argue that you can be a Christian and not go to church. I argue that this statement becomes less and less true the longer you stay away from the Church. It cannot be right that the world be littered with "severed body parts" when we are meant to be together! As Paul writes in 1 Corinthians 12:20-21, "As it is, there are many parts, but one body. The eye cannot say to the hand, "I don't need you!" And the head cannot say to the feet, "I don't need you!"

The isolation from the Church many believers are experiencing is exacerbated by their misunderstanding of what the Bible says about church. Church isn't a club or a place to peddle your own agendas. It is not a political party where you can take a vote of "no confidence" when you disagree with the leadership. Church is a gathering of people at various levels of maturity and development. Church is designed to "rub you up the wrong way." Church was made to be a place of maturity where you learn to act and react like our Lord. Church is a place where are to learn to rhythmically and easily work together.[88] Church is a place where we learn to flow together. All of this encapsulates God's people being built together into a spiritual house.

Scripture is really clear on this point. Hebrews 10:25 says, "Let us not give up meeting together, as some are in the habit of doing, but let us encourage one another and all the more as you see the Day approaching." As parts of Christ's body we have a responsibility to meet together regularly. The writer is correcting a habit that was forming in the early Church, just as it is a problem today. All kinds of wrong doctrine begins to emerge when people drift away from the Church. All sorts of bad behaviour and attitudes begin to form. People disconnected from the body are like little children, tossed to and fro by waves.[89] They demonstrate immaturity and are "blown here and there by the cunning and craftiness of men in deceitful scheming."[90] The Bible is clear that we need to be in fellowship with other Christians and to meet regularly together.

Some scholars interpret this reference to the "approaching day" as meaning the first day of the week[91] or "The Lord's Day".[92] Others are split, some saying it refers to the Day of Judgement and others that it referred to the imminent fall of Jerusalem. However we interpret its meaning, it gives me an opportunity to make the point that there is a day each week that belongs to God, a day for the body to gather and worship Him corporately, and to hear the Word of God preached. It is a day to serve one another in the body and welcome those who are as yet unconnected. Many churches meet on days other than Sunday for good reasons – I'm not campaigning for a return to Sabbath Law. The point is, we are meant to gather the body together to connect and engage. This comes as a fresh revelation to many who feel disconnected but don't want to be, who feel isolated but want to belong. This is what the body of Christ is all about! Gathering in all who are disconnected from its Head.

Learning to flow together

I love the biblical picture of a body to represent Christ's Church. We see a sense of mutual dependency. A body needs all its members in order to be whole and function correctly. Each part has to do its part. Not only is there a negative effect on a toe if it is cut off, but it has a knock on effect on the rest of the body. It is amazing how difficult it is to walk properly when you are missing a toe!

As church leaders we must be committed to preaching these truths if we are to see a body that knows how to function and flow together. It's not a magic formula and there will always be those who disagree, but if you preach the truth long enough, eventually you will see a body coming together where once there was only disconnected parts.

Ephesians 5:21 says, "Submit to one another out of reverence for Christ." The Message translates it this way: "Out of respect for Christ, be courteously reverent to one another." Regardless of the explanation people don't like the word "submit." It has become popular to remove it from marriage vows too. But it is a biblical word rich with meaning!

The word "submit" means to "put yourself under" or "allow yourself to be subdued."[93] Scripture refers to it as something we are to do to one another. The Bible doesn't advocate it being a one-way street. In our church we express this scripture by saying we must, "learn how to flow together with each other." This is at the heart of all our initiatives. The Message version's translation of Ephesians 4:13 is particularly evocative: "… working within Christ's body, the church, until we're all moving rhythmically and easily with each other, efficient and graceful in response to God's Son, fully mature adults, fully developed within and without, fully alive like Christ."

I love this picture of a healthy church! We are to move "rhythmically and easily with each other" – healthy people finding meaning in the Church who learn to be "graceful in response to God's Son" as they find their function. From here we go on to become fully mature, fully developed and fully alive! This passage redefines for me what Christian maturity is all about. It has little to do with our knowledge of the Scriptures and much more to do with our willingness to move rhythmically and easily with others for the cause of Christ's kingdom.

Most problems in church are caused by immature people starting fights and causing division. They confuse their chronological age with their spiritual maturity! If only people would learn the grace of flowing together and submitting to one another we'd see our churches become so much more effective in winning cities.

Learning how to flow together can only be accomplished if we *are together*. If people disconnect from the Church, they have no place in which to practice the vital art of flowing together in unity. Paul, writing to the church in Rome, asked God to give them a spirit of unity amongst themselves. He wanted to encourage them both to be together and to be in unity.

"May the God who gives endurance and encouragement give you a spirit of unity among yourselves as you follow Christ Jesus, so that with one heart and mouth you may glorify the God and Father of our Lord Jesus Christ. Accept one another, then, just as Christ accepted you, in order to bring praise to God." (Romans 15:5-7)

Paul encouraged the church to have one heart and speak with one mouth as they glorified God – in other words, to "say the same thing" and move together with a clear and unifying vision. Finally, he exhorted the church to work with one another and honour one another.[94] We can't do any of this stuff if we are disengaged from the Church!

A healthy body gives people a chance to serve together. By "serving" I don't mean occasional volunteering but actually doing what God has put you here to do – expressing your function in the body. Psalm 110:3 (NKJV) says, "Your people shall be volunteers in the day of your power." The NIV translates this verse, "Your troops will be willing on your day of battle." This willingness of heart springs from a heart that is connected to God and His House. This spirit of service happens naturally when people find themselves in right relationship with God and are connected as part of His Church.

Many leaders are scared to preach to people about their need to serve in the church. They feel like they are putting a burden on people by asking them to do stuff. No! Leaders, you are helping people fulfil their destiny by finding their function in the body. Don't stop exhorting people to serve! Your role is to, "… prepare God's people for works of service, so that the body of Christ may be built up" (Ephesians 4:12) or as The Message puts it, "to train Christ's followers in skilled servant work, working within Christ's body, the church."

Leaders, as Ephesians 4 gift ministries, are to train people in "skilled servant work" within the Church. They are to help believers learn how to flow together with each other; to help them produce the "graceful response" that will result in them becoming fully mature followers of Christ and fully alive in Him. As Mark Batterson in his book *Primal*[95] puts it, we are to "not just act like Christians but *react* like Christians."

Romans 12 talks about giving people opportunities to serve, allowing them to do what God has graced them to do. Notice it says that when we are a part of Christ's body we are "excellently formed and marvellously functioning". I think that would be a phenomenal way to be described as a person! This is why we should never downplay how significant it is to serve in church life. Discipleship happens when people join teams and serve together with one another. We are transformed by serving others in church. Discipleship doesn't take place simply by preaching great messages, or by taking someone through a course (both of which may be necessary), it happens when people serve side by side with others.

The bits of the body you don't see

One of the lessons we are bound to learn as we seek to serve in God's House is that there is a big difference between "prominence" and "significance". Even the smallest, apparently mundane job, is significant in the body of Christ. But there are those people who mistakenly look for prominence rather than significance. They want to be "seen" rather than simply "serve".

I vividly remember one couple who began attending our church. They made an appointment to see me. I asked them how they were fitting in and inquired whether they were enjoying being a part of the church. They said they loved the worship and the teaching on Sundays. I asked them where they wanted to serve. They didn't respond clearly and were a bit hard to read, so I suggested they serve in our First Impressions (greeting) team. They replied, "Oh, we've been there and done that for thirty years!" "Okay," I replied, "how about in hospitality or with the children? Or perhaps you could help out with stage management?" I got the same response. They had been there, done that, got the T-shirt. Eventually I got their drift. They wanted a more "prominent" position. I asked what they would like to do. The husband said he had been an elder in his last church and thought that could work well here too. His wife said she had a prophetic ministry and wondered why we didn't have an open microphone at the front of the auditorium so she could prophesy. I graciously responded by saying that neither of these positions were open to them at this juncture and encouraged them to come to one of our "new to church" parties to get a better understanding of our church. I encouraged them to be humble and just serve in the house wherever they were needed at first. This comment didn't go down well. Sadly they wanted to be seen to be important. They had missed the significance of simply serving and allowing God to develop and release their gifting. They had lost the spirit of Ecclesiastes 9:10 which says, "Whatever your hand finds to do, do it with all your might."

In the physical body there are parts you see and parts you don't see, but they are all equally important. So it is in Christ's body. Much work needs to be done behind the scenes, without which the parts that people do see could not function.

My service within the body is leading, communicating, casting vision and developing other leaders. Some serve by working with the children and others serve by caring for our youth. There are those who serve behind a computer making media and some who serve by standing behind a video camera. There are the people who do stage management and those who set up the venue and pull it down at night. There are so many aspects to the body of Christ! But note that each part gets its meaning from the body as a whole, not the other way round. What you have to offer is wonderful, but it won't give you meaning. Only as you express your gift in the context of the body will you find meaning. I love it on a Sunday evening when our pack down team is working away and someone shouts out, "Seven people came to Christ tonight!" In response, everyone else shouts out. Then someone will say, "They couldn't have made it happen without us!" This might sound proud or arrogant to some. It's not! It is absolutely true! These people have found meaning in Christ's body and have discovered their function. You must find yours!

Notes

85. Psalm 92:13
86. 1 Peter 2:5
87. 1 Corinthians 12:13
88. Ephesians 4:12 The Message
89. Ephesians 4:14
90. Ibid.
91. Acts 20:7, 1 Corinthians 16:1-2
92. Revelation 1:10
93. Strong's Concordance
94. Romans 12:10
95. Mark Batterson, *Primal*, Multnomah Publishers Inc., 2009.

Part Three

THE 7 CHARACTERISTICS

OF A 21ST CENTURY

RELENTNESS

CHURCH

11

RELENTLESS CHURCH – REVIVALIST, PROPHETIC, EVANGELISTIC

> "O Lord, I have heard thy speech, and was afraid: O Lord, revive thy work in the midst of the years, in the midst of the years make known; in wrath remember mercy."
> (Habakkuk 3:2 KJV)

Over the next three chapters we will look at seven traits that characterise and, for me, sum up what the *relentless church* should look like. I offer these seven aspects to inspire hope, encouragement and positive action on the part of churches and church leaders everywhere.

Characteristic 1: a place of revival

A world in crisis demands a Church in revival! All over the world a great darkness has covered the earth (Isaiah 60:2). Let me say, without too much religious fanaticism, that it does appear we are living in the last days. The time for the return of Christ hastens upon us. Jesus is coming back soon!

But currently the world is in a huge complicated mess. Natural disasters are now occurring dozens of times a year and wars in different parts of the world are beamed into our living rooms. Man continues to practice inhumanity on his fellow man as we invent new and novel ways to inflict pain on one another. A world in such crisis demands a living, breathing Church full of fire. We're not going to cut it with some sleepy, irrelevant, otherworldly group of people stuck in a time warp, hoping something will happen.

It bothers me when I think of people sitting around singing songs and prophesying to each other while communities are going to Hell.

It disturbs me to hear of church conflicts and petty disagreements in the body.

It upsets me when Christians become embroiled in petty political manoeuvring to get their own way while unimaginable horrors are taking place on our doorsteps.

We need to get beyond our infighting and squabbles and get some perspective here. We need to allow the Holy Spirit to revive our cold hearts and begin a revival in us individually and then our churches! Only then will our churches be transformed into hubs of revival that can answer the needs of our broken communities. The reformer John Knox cried out in prayer, "Give me Scotland or I die!" and Mary Queen of Scots declared she was more afraid of Knox's prayers than an army of ten thousand. We need to capture a similar spirit and heart for our communities, until we can cry out a prayer like his for our town, city and nation.

Although the prophet Isaiah spoke of a great darkness on the land, the main theme of those verses is one of hope:

"Arise, shine, for your light has come, and the glory of the LORD rises upon you. See, darkness covers the earth and thick darkness is over the peoples, but the LORD rises upon you and his glory appears over you. Nations will come to your light, and kings to the brightness of your dawn." (Isaiah 60:1-3)

The last days are not about doom and gloom for the Church as so many seem to think. For the Church they are full of God's promises. More than any other time in history, this is our time to shine! We are called to be the people of God in revival for a land under the tyranny of darkness.

Listen to the prophecy of Haggai 2:9:

"'The glory of this present house will be greater than the glory of the former house,' says the LORD Almighty."

The Church has much to look forward to.

It is my deep conviction that we have barely begun to see the influence of the Church on our societies. We've only just begun to see the Church grow in both numbers and in impact. We've only just begun to see the transforming power of the Church on society today. The Church is emerging!

God has called us to be a people who are filled with His Holy Spirit and are vibrantly full of life. He has poured out His Spirit upon us so we can be full of His energy, vital, alive and effervescent. This is the prevailing Church – a Church alive with the sound of new Christians; a Church characterised by passion, exuberance and enthusiasm.

In our times the Church must be on fire, in revival and spiritually alert. It is our responsibility to lead people into ever refreshing experiences with God and His Holy Spirit, so that we maintain the spirit of revival.

Characteristic 2: powerful and prophetic

Acts 2:17-19 gives us a picture of the 21st Century *relentless* Church:

> "In the last days, I will pour out my Spirit on all people. Your sons and daughters will prophesy, your young men will see visions, your old men will dream dreams. Even on my servants, both men and women, I will pour out my Spirit in those days, and they will prophesy. I will show wonders in the heaven above and signs on the earth below."

It is a Church that is both filled with spiritual *power* and highly *prophetic*:

Powerful: the relentless Church is made up of "holy warriors", but not warriors in the militaristic sense. Occasionally the New Testament will refer to us being like "soldiers"[96] as it draws a spiritual analogy, but some people get carried away with this. I don't think it bodes well in today's culture to over egg the militaristic parallels when thinking about the Church. The kind of "power" Jesus wants us to have is the kind He referred to when He said that He would baptise us with the Holy Spirit and fire.[97] Acts 1:8 indicates that this power is given to us so we can be witnesses for Christ.

Prophetic: the relentless Church is also prophetic – prophetic in the sense of communicating God's message to those who are lost with insight and relevance. Being a prophetic church is about …

> … visualising the kind of city you want to live in, in the next 20 years.
> … keeping firmly rooted in "today" as we speak about what tomorrow will look like.
> … not allowing pie in the sky, nebulous words, but boldly communicating God's plan for our city, community and beyond.

... believing that God loves our cities and wants the best for them.

... becoming what God intends for us as a group of people.

To truly be prophetic we first need to understand the times we live in. Many churches are stuck in a dreadful time warp and simply don't engage in or understand the world around them. As a result their prophetic voice is muted.

Part of being a prophetic community has to do with empowering and releasing younger people to be all they were meant to be for their generation. If we don't have a growing group of young people in our churches we are on a collision course with destruction – purely from a church growth point of view – and our "voice" to society will be ineffective. Our young people are a window to the world for us. They help us connect with "today" and are a breath of fresh, creative air! If we want to reach out to young people, then who better to do that than young people themselves? I love the thought that every week people of all ages get saved in our church. It thrills me to see how many people's lives are powerfully altered by exposure to Jesus and His Church. This is being prophetic!

Characteristic 3: salt and light to the world

Colossians 4:6 gives us the following guidance:

> "Let your conversation be always full of grace, seasoned with salt, so that you may know how to answer everyone." (Colossians 4:6)

And I love this translation of Matthew 5:13-16: in The Message:

> "Let me tell you why you are here. You're here to be salt-seasoning that brings out the God-flavours of this earth. If you lose your saltiness, how will people taste godliness? You've lost your usefulness and will end up in the garbage. Here's another way to put it: You're here to be light, bringing

out the God-colours in the world. God is not a secret to be kept. We're going public with this, as public as a city on a hill. If I make you light-bearers, you don't think I'm going to hide you under a bucket, do you? I'm putting you on a light stand. Now that I've put you there on a hilltop, on a light stand—shine! Keep open house; be generous with your lives. By opening up to others, you'll prompt people to open up with God, this generous Father in heaven."

It's good to remind ourselves frequently of exactly why we are here!

The Church (meaning you and me) exists to be *salt* to bring out the God-flavours of the Earth. It's profoundly simple: we are here to add flavour to, enhance and improve people's lives. We're here to highlight God. We're here to spice up the world and add to, not detract from, the great taste of Jesus. We are here to bring out the God flavours all around us.

Salt has two main qualities: to add flavour and to preserve. Salt is used to make food palatable, pleasant and prevent it from going off. Why is it that some make the Gospel unpalatable by saying things like, "We need to make it hard for people to come to Jesus. Then we know that they are really saved!"

Christianity is not a list of rules, but a vibrant relationship with God. Christianity is not a religion that seeks to control people's lives with laws and regulations. We cannot expect people to live like a Christian when they have never connected with Jesus. Instead of making it hard for people to come to Jesus with our customs, traditions and barriers to entry, we should be living attractive, Holy Spirit filled lives that draw people's interest in Christ. We don't want our faith to appear to others like a list of religious regulations.

We are the salt of the earth motivated to bring out the God-flavours in the world around us. Our lives are meant to help others to "taste and see" that God is good. We need to teach more about being salt. We need to explain to those who follow Christ that our lives are supposed to be attractive, filled with wonder. We are called to live lives that are appealing, pleasant and delightful. Even when we go through tough times we can demonstrate to others strength, peace and a calm assurance of faith. If we live like this, Jesus says we will "prompt others to open up to our generous Father in Heaven."

We are also here to be light as well as salt, to bring out the God-colours in the world. We're here to be "light bearers" – to shine, to be transparent, to live generous lives that touch others. The Church should be a place of lavish colour that shows off God's genius. The Church should be a place where we demonstrate that Jesus is not black and white and two dimensional, but a richly coloured, three dimensional, living breathing Christ who wants to connect with us in the real world.

We are here to reveal to a waiting world the colours of Heaven, the uniqueness of God's creative work in the life of every man, woman and child that walks the planet. We are the only Christ that some people will ever see. As Paul the apostle wrote,

> "God has chosen to make known among the Gentiles the glorious riches of this mystery, which is Christ in you, the hope of glory." (Colossians 1:27)

God has chosen to reveal *us* to the world, to reveal the glorious riches of Christ *in us!* We are like letters waiting to be read by all those whose lives we touch, as 2 Corinthians 3:2-4 says:

> "You yourselves are our letter, written on our hearts, known and read by everybody. You show that you are a letter from Christ, the result of our ministry, written not with ink but with the Spirit of the living God, not on tablets of stone but on tablets of human hearts. Such confidence as this is ours through Christ before God."

I am reminded of a young woman who came along to our church. For seven months she attended regularly, was part of a small group and served on a team faithfully. Here's the thing: she had yet to surrender her life to Christ! One morning, I remember it vividly, at the conclusion of my message I gave people an opportunity to receive Jesus and she put her hand up. I was a bit astounded. She said to one of our leaders, "I wanted to make sure you Christians were what you said you were. I wanted to make sure you were genuine. If you were, then it was true what you said about Jesus. When I was sure, then I wanted to commit my life to Christ and follow Him for the rest of my life!"

WOW! What a story!

It remains our responsibility to *"...be being full of the Holy Spirit"*[98] so we can bring out the God-colours in the world around us! God is not a secret to be kept. It's time to go public with this. Tell everyone you know about Jesus and if you must, use words! Our job is to create a culture and an environment where there exists a reflection of the kingdom of Heaven. Let's work hard to be salt and light and to make our churches a little bit of Heaven on Earth. Let's create atmosphere in which the Holy Spirit can move with ease!

Notes

96. 2 Timothy 2:3
97. Luke 3:16
98. Ephesians 5:18

12

RELENTLESS CHURCH – CONNECTED, SALVATION-ORIENTATED, SPIRITUAL, CONTEMPORARY

Characteristic 4: in the world, but not of the world

When Jesus prayed for His disciples in John 17:14-19 He made the following request of His Father:

> "My prayer is not that you take them out of the world but that you protect them from the evil one. They are not of the world, even as I am not of it. Sanctify them by the truth; your word is truth. As you sent me into the world, I have sent them into the world. For them I sanctify myself, that they too may be truly sanctified."

Jesus' great and potent prayer stands for all those who would follow Him, and His desire today is that we would not abandon our responsibility to touch the world with His love. Let's unpack these verses:

1. Not taken out of the world, but protected from the evil one

I see a great many "other worldly" Christians today, "super-Christians" who have sought to extricate themselves from anything to do with the world. The most extreme example would be moving into a monastery and becoming a type of hermit. I meet some believers who don't watch TV, would never go to a movie theatre, and never listen to the radio. There are some who refuse to read anything other than the Bible, not even a newspaper. This isn't what Jesus intended!

Thankfully, I am also seeing a generation who is quite at home walking the streets of our world. They are bold, sassy and confident. They know that if we are to reach the world we live in, we can't do it from a distance. Up close and personal is what we want. We need to understand the philosophy and morality being sold by today's media in film and music. We need to be on the same wavelength as those in the world so that we can speak to them in terms they understand, not "Christianese".

I believe it is only as we become familiar with the language of media that we can reach people with the eternal message of Christ. We need to connect with people like Jesus, joining in with *their* conversations and talking along with them. Clearly this means not sticking our heads in the sand and ignoring the world around us!

2. We are IN, but not OF the world, sanctified by the truth of God's Word

What does this mean for us today? It means we don't need to become prostitutes to reach prostitutes. We don't need to smoke marijuana to reach druggies. Neither do we need to lower our morals to reach those with no morals. Jesus was abundantly clear in His prayer: we are not *of* this world. We are not a people infected by the spirit of this age. We've been born again by the Holy Spirit and are people of another kingdom. We've been sanctified, separated, made holy by Christ and His Word. But we are *in the world*. We cannot separate or extricate ourselves from it. Our goal is to live here with a "different spirit" that is the source of our attractiveness.

3. We have been sent into the world as Christ was sent into the world, to proclaim the goodness of God

Our job here on Earth is to proclaim a kingdom beyond people's wildest dreams! Jesus commanded us to "Go into all the world…"

Jesus became flesh and blood so that He could relate to broken humanity. Like Him we need to be "flesh and blood" people – fully human, though infused with the power of His Spirit; vitally connected to the world but reflecting the glorious power of Heaven. Don't be other worldly. Don't try to be super-spiritual. Try not to be answering questions no one is asking. Learn to listen. It is amazing how people will often lead us into talking about God without us trying.

Most of my "divine connections" happen in coffee shops or when I'm out getting my hair cut. The other day my hairdresser, wanting to connect with me, asked, "Did you ever see that Mel Gibson movie about Jesus?"

"Yes," I replied. "Did you enjoy it?"

"Yes," he said. "I loved that part right at the end when He came back to life and looked out over the scenery."

"Yeah," I said, "pretty amazing, eh?" I looked at him and asked, "You know what that means, don't you? He is still alive, never to die again, and He did it all for us."

He stared in amazement and finally commented: "Awesome!"

It wasn't a forced or difficult discussion!

Talking with people who are not yet connected with Jesus should always take precedence over talking to those who are. This slightly annoys my more "religious" friends when frequently I stop talking to them to turn and focus on someone who is unsaved. Recently I was sitting in Starbucks with a Christian friend when a young man came over to us. He looked a little lost and miserable. I looked up and complimented him on his great afro haircut and he immediately brightened up, thanking me. He was looking for a seat and there we no free tables so he asked if he could join us. I agreed immediately!

Within fifteen minutes my religious friend got tired and left. I ended up chatting to this young man for a further forty-five minutes. He was wide open to hearing about Jesus. We talked about church, about Jesus, and even his business plan. I loved his ideas and we got along famously. At the end he thanked me profusely for spending time with him and mentioned that a friend of his had been talking to him about going to church too. I left him with a lot to think about.

It bothers me when I see a group of people calling themselves Christians who attend a church but are not involved in the lives of the people in its community. I'm not even talking about social aid – providing food or clothing for those in need – I'm talking about simply making our presence known in the everyday lives of the people around us with the purpose of seeking and saving the lost. Many Christian are simply "invisible", hiding behind walled building and keeping their lives a secret. But the Church Jesus is building is one where people are comfortable being part of the world and are not afraid of it.

I love that Jesus is portrayed in Scripture as a friend of every-day people. It was something for which He was heavily criticised by the religious leaders. But Jesus didn't care. He loved people and was determined to hang out with them, especially those considered the dregs of society by the religious! Yet, He was no slouch when it came to saying the hard stuff people needed to hear about their lives. There was never any hint of compromise.

Characteristic 5: a place of salvation

"I tell you that in the same way there will be more rejoicing in heaven over one sinner who repents than over ninety-nine righteous persons who do not need to repent." (Luke 15:7)

Just as there is a great outpouring of joy when a couple celebrate the birth of a child and the whole family joins in, from brothers and sisters to grandparents to extended family, so there is widespread joy in the house of God when a person gets born again. There is no greater source of joy in God's house than when someone gets saved. This joy helps to create an atmosphere of celebration; it generates enthusiasm and excitement.

For any church to be truly healthy it must be seeing people get saved regularly. God's house is an awesome place because it is a house of salvation, a place of transformation; a place where people are reconciled with Him! Church may not always suit our personal preferences – we may not care for the noise, the style of music or the preacher – but if people are getting saved then God is in the house!

I remember when I was pastoring in Melbourne, Australia. My church was quite radical for its time. We had a rock band leading worship, which in the 1980s was unheard of. When we started the church a few older people from the area began attending it, but when they heard the music they left, rapidly! This disgruntled group went to another church that was pastored by my mentor and long term friend, Philip Hills. On the first morning these folks attended the church, Phil greeted them asking why they were there. One guy said, "We've left that church. It's a circus and Tom Rawls is the chief clown!" Phil rebuked him and said, "Hey! People are getting saved there. Let's have no more criticism!"

Of course, I felt vindicated by this, but do you know what? It is the frequency of salvations that vindicates any church's existence. Are people getting saved in your church? Are they maturing into disciples? Are people meeting deeply with God? Is your church growing because of new converts, rather than people moving church? If so, then don't worry about anything else!

I ask the question again: what validates a church? It's not your denominational tag. It's not the size of your congregation. It's not how lovely your building is, the quality of your programmes or the slickness of your multimedia. It is simply whether or not people are coming to Christ because of you.

The atmosphere of a church is affected by people coming to Christ. A churches mood is lifted when people are getting saved. We get what Peter called "an inexpressible and glorious joy!" There are no rules or formulas for this: I'm not prescribing that there should be a certain number of people saved each month or each year. We just need to make sure people are coming to Christ, because when they do it will lead to even more people connecting with Christ. New Christians know a lot of people and they can't help telling others about their discovery!

I regularly hear leaders say, "We're not seeing people get saved." I ask them, "As leaders are you providing people with an opportunity to respond to Christ?" It sounds basic, but the fact is we are often lacking in intentionality and get so wrapped up in our programmes that we forget to make room, constantly and consistently, to give people the opportunity to respond to Jesus. In every one of our church services we have a part dedicated to giving people the chance to say YES to Jesus.

Every aspect of our church – the services, the advertising and marketing – should be viewed from the perspective of those who are not yet connected with Christ. Our traditions and rituals should either be explained or chucked out. We must recognise that the mission of the Church is to reach people, influence culture and build the future! This is the kind of Church Jesus is building today. It is a forward-moving Church that is making sure it will exist for another generation of people.

Characteristic 6: a spiritual house

1 Peter 2:4–5 says,

> "As you come to him, the living Stone, rejected by men but chosen by God and precious to him you also, like living stones, are being built into a *spiritual house* to be a holy priesthood, offering spiritual sacrifices acceptable to God through Jesus Christ."

The Church that Jesus is building is a spiritual house. I love the present continuous tense used here: *"… are being built …"*. It tells us that the work is not finished yet – it's a work in progress. The task of us cooperating and co-working with Christ and each other is our lifelong vocation.

We are reminded that the foundation of this spiritual house is Jesus. As Paul wrote, what other foundation can we have than Jesus?[99]

This is why it is so vital that as church leaders we keep Christ as the central focus of everything we do. If Christ is central we don't get caught up in how great our worship is, how awesome our media is or how wonderful our hosting team is. We are constantly bringing the church back to how awesome Christ is. I like the line from the Hillsong song, *Freedom is Here*[100]: "Everything comes alive in my life as I lift you higher." It thrills me to know that there is only room for one superstar in the Church and His name is Jesus. Real problems emerge when you allow any other personality to dominate and achieve a greatness which rivals that of Christ.

This passage also tells us about who we are. Being a spiritual house is about being a part of something bigger. We are not merely individuals. Get this point: the Church is not a collection of random people, all with their own ideas of how it works and fits together. The Church is so much more than that. We are being built together as a spiritual house.

This verse reminds us that everything flows out of relationship. It all starts with our foundational relationship with Jesus, but from there we are bound together with each other, cemented into relationships with those around us. You can spot people who don't get "cemented" into the wall of God's house – they don't allow themselves to get fully involved in what God is doing. They deny themselves the privilege of helping to build His house and the joy of serving.

One of our leaders relayed to me the story of an encounter he'd had with someone who had been attending our church for about a year. He innocently asked a lady why she hadn't joined a team yet. She responded, "I only come to this church because of my husband!" End of conversation! So my friend turned to her husband and asked why he hadn't gotten involved in a team. His response was quite angry as he reeled off a number of excuses. Needless to say this couple didn't hang around for long. People who don't want to be build into the spiritual house will always wander off eventually.

There are many who stay on the fringe of church life and are not "plugged in" as living stones. They are missing out on so much. Church is not a spectator sport, it's a place where you have to actively engage in order to get the best out of it and put your best into it. Everything really does flow out of relationship. We never hear it said that the world depends on *acquaintances!* Even business experts recognise that everything hinges on relationships. The spiritual house is all about friendships, accountability partners, peers and leadership. All these layers and with their different kinds of relationships is what we need in life to help us to flourish and grow.

Look at any building site and you will see bricks sitting around in piles, waiting to become part of a wall. As church leaders we need to work on strategies that move people out of "piles" sitting in a corner to be part of a wall somewhere in the structure where they fit right in. It's not going to happen by chance, we need to be intentional. We need to reconnect with Christ's vision for His Church, remind ourselves of the Master Builder's plans, just as any builder will keep on looking at his plans to keep in mind what he is working to create. When we constantly come back to what Jesus intends His Church to look like, then we will deliberately and carefully work with Him as co-labourers to make the Church of His dreams a reality.

Characteristic 7: culturally contemporary

The final characteristic of relentless Church is that it is relevant to its contemporary society. As science fiction writer Alvin Toffler once said, "The illiterates of the 21st century will not be those who cannot read and write, but those who cannot learn, unlearn, and relearn." And as the writer of 1 Chronicles noted, we need to be like the "… men of Issachar, who understood the times and knew what Israel should do" (1 Chronicles 12:31).

Listen to this tongue in cheek article from www.wittenburgdoor.com which voted Buffy the Vampire Slayer as "Theologian of the year" in 2002:

> "Perilous times call for bold theology. Let's face it. Evil is running rampant … The ozone layer is perforated, glaciers are melting, terrorists are everywhere, crazies set wildfires that denude the landscape. Generation X passes the baton to Generation Y, adolescence is still hell, AND THERE'S ONLY ONE LETTER LEFT! We need someone who can not only deconstruct the problem of evil, but kick its backside; someone with a preternatural sense of comic timing and an eye for fashion. We need Buffy."[101]

The author of the article, identified as Skippy R, is right in my opinion! *Perilous times do call for a bold theology.* For too many the Jesus that the Church represents is a Jesus who has been, "domesticated, de-clawed and kept under wraps."[102] People are looking for a bold, audacious Christ to follow and people are looking for a courageous theology in tune with "today".

From sunsets to movie sets God is speaking

St Thomas Aquinas, a 13th Century priest and theologian, argued that wherever people saw the qualities of mercy, justice, prudence and hope, then named or not, Christ was present. People can "sense" God's invisible qualities in everything from a stunning sunset to a thought-provoking Hollywood film. The fact is, people are searching for the truth. Men and women are constantly looking for purpose, meaning and understanding in their lives. Never in the history of mankind have people been so interested in the spiritual dimension of life as they are now.

Chris Carter, the creator of the cult TV Show *The X-Files*, says this about the show: "I think faith informs almost every episode. I am a sceptic by nature … but I really have a desire, as I believe we all do, to find a reason to believe, to have my scepticism tested."

We recognise this hunt, this desperation to find a reason to believe in something. God's presence is felt in the world even if it is not acknowledged by all. He has dropped too many hints not to be noticed. His unique fingerprints are everywhere. We see evidence of His DNA in the most unexpected places. God has not abandoned modern culture, nor is He silent. Pop culture remains a domain where people can find God. This means that we should utilise it and cooperate with it, rather than fight it.

The worst ever advertising campaign

The image of the Church so often portrayed in the media tends to work two ways: either we are seen as an old fashioned, outmoded institution, stuck in the past, or as wacky, extreme and eccentric on the fringes of society.

The Church's challenge is to use the 21st Century as its backdrop and to be at home "in the world" without appearing either desperately dull or slightly insane. Like missionaries, we need to learn the language of contemporary culture and learn how to communicate the message of Jesus to a "today" generation without diluting or compromising it.

Jesus is solid like a rock, trustworthy and faithful. His nature and character is unchanging from generation to generation. The writer to the Hebrews says He is "the same yesterday *today* and forever." Yet, He invades time to demonstrate His love and salvation to our present generation. Not only has He invaded time, but He has embedded Himself *into* our times, our culture and our world. God has not forsaken the culture and society of today. On the contrary, His presence is seen and felt by all those who look a little closer. Jesus has not forsaken the world. He has not stayed behind in some other decade or century, leaving us to fend for ourselves in the 21st Century. He hasn't grown fond of the Victorian age and abandoned us! So we too need a 21st Century Church with a 21st Century perspective.

Craig Detweiler and Barry Taylor write in their book, *A Matrix of Meaning: Finding God in Popular Culture,*

"We embrace pop culture because we believe it offers a refreshing, alternative route to a Jesus ... As the Christian Church has often adopted the role of moral policeman, pop culture has assumed the role of spiritual revolutionary, subverting and frustrating those religious authorities who desperately cling to black-and-white answers in an increasingly grey world ... We believe a bold, ancient, radical Christ stands on the sidelines of the culture wars, waiting 'with arms wide open,' eager to engage our hearts, our minds, and our culture." [103]

From the narratives of the Gospels to the actions of the early followers of Christ, Jesus is radical! Jesus Christ is bold and fresh, incredibly touchable and accessible right here in our 21st Century. He simply cannot be contained! We need to abandon our mild mannered "Clark Kent" Christianity and let loose the radical power of the Gospel, doing all we can to be contemporary, audacious and attractive.

Notes

99. 1 Corinthians 3:11
100. Hillsong United from *Tear Down the Walls* By Skippy R., Door magazine, issue no.183, Sept/Oct 2002
101. By Skippy R., Door magazine, issue no.183, Sept/Oct 2002
102. Craig Detweiler and Barry Taylor, A Matrix of Meanings: Finding God in Pop Culture, Revell, 2003
103. Ibid.

Part Four

REDISCOVERING JESUS

13

JESUS – THE HEART OF OUR MESSAGE

"The essential teachings of Jesus... were literally revolutionary, and will always remain so if they are taken seriously."
—Herbert Muller (American Historian)

"No one can read the gospels without feeling the actual presence of Jesus.
His personality pulsates in every word. No myth is filled with such life."
—Albert Einstein

"I am an historian, I am not a believer, but I must confess as a historian that this penniless preacher from Nazareth is irrevocably the very centre of history. Jesus Christ is easily the most dominant figure in all history."
—H.G. Wells (Science fiction writer)

From Leonardo to Michelangelo, renaissance artists painted religious scenes. Among their depictions of angels and demons, the Madonna and child and many of the Saints, were prolific works with Jesus as their subject. But much as I love these artists and admire their craft, their portrayal of Jesus doesn't line up with what I see in the Bible. These images, preserved down the centuries have, I believe, gone a long way to skewing people's perception of Jesus, our Lord. We need to restore an accurate view of the *real Jesus* – powerful, triumphant, a warrior and great leader, who is the foundation of the might, relentless, unstoppable Church He is building.

Most would agree we now live in a "post Christian" era in Europe. The Church is no longer an institution with political power or moral gravitas. There are few who have the opportunity to stand in their parliament and declare the word of the Lord. Instead, our job is to build relationships and earn the permission to speak. Some in our secularised society say the Church has no business being in existence. Some are angry with the Church and others antagonistic towards the concept of there being a God – such as scientist Richard Dawkins, who paid good money to launch an advertising campaign saying, "There's probably no God."

My desire then, is that we prayerfully enlist the person of the Holy Spirit to assist us to raise the profile of Jesus Christ and in turn show the true glory of His Church. Since Jesus is the foundation of the Church, the very centre of the universe, the most important figure in all of history, we must educate and encourage a deeper appreciation of who He is and somehow bridge the gap between the 1st century view of Him and the 21st century view. A Church must arise now with grace and power to spread the kingdom's culture upon this sin-soaked earth; to preach Jesus Christ and Him crucified. As Jesus Himself asserted,

> "But I, when I am lifted up from the earth, will draw all men to myself." (John 12:32)

Our context is vital to understand

As we look at the 1st Century spread of the gospel, Corinth or even Rome, is a better context for us than Jerusalem. If we were to study the expansion of the Jerusalem church we would not understand how the power of the gospel impacted those outside the Jewish faith.

Men like Paul took the good news to every place in Asia Minor and Western Europe, including Corinth and Rome under mandate from Christ:

> "For this is what the Lord has commanded us: 'I have made you a light for the Gentiles, that you may bring salvation to the ends of the earth.'" (Acts 13:47)

Corinth was the sex capital of Asia Minor, a place of pagan rituals and notorious immorality. It was the capital city of Achaia, a region and city re-founded by Julius Caesar and a centre for Greek philosophers. It was also a place where many Jews had fled during the reign of Roman Emperor Claudius, hence Paul's initial outreach was to them. But soon his ministry went beyond the Jewish community and he began to speak to gentiles with great boldness empowered by the Spirit.

Much like Europe today, Corinth and Rome posed a great challenge to Paul and his team as they sought to preach the good news of Jesus there. The similarities to our society today are striking, yet encouraging, because Paul and his team were successful in planting large and significant churches there. Corinth and Rome were pre-Christian: there was no understanding of Jesus there. Most people had no knowledge of the Scriptures; most had never heard of Jesus Christ; most had never seen a Bible; most had never heard of the possibility of having a relationship with the God of creation. Much like Europe of today, Corinth and Rome were hotbeds of darkness and sin. Paul and his band of preachers had a huge task before them. But by the Holy Spirit's power progress was made and the Church was established. God helped Paul and He will help us.

Content

Though the context of the 21st Century is staggering and complex it should never affect our content. We have seen that our communication must be relevant and contemporary, but let's make sure we don't dilute or compromise our message.

Paul said in 1 Corinthians 2 that he "did not come with eloquence or superior wisdom". His resolve was to know nothing except "Jesus Christ and Him crucified". Paul made Christ his central and constant theme. This was his determination and it should be ours. Paul knew the Greeks had a penchant for philosophy, intellectual debate and the subtleties of language, but he was determined not to be seduced by their Gnostic ideas and their need for existential explanations. He made sure that his messages were based around one grand theme: Jesus Christ, His death and resurrection – communicated not with clever words and arguments, but with a raw demonstration of the power of God.

This message Paul sought to communicate *relied* upon a God of miracles, a God of power and substance. The core of his message was the reality of supernatural power. This is why Paul professed to come "in weakness and fear, and with much trembling." Paul was a highly educated, skilled orator, but this wasn't about him! He didn't come to show off his brilliant personality or flaunt his educational credentials. He was there to unfold the miraculous message about a God of love who had prepared the world for the arrival of His Son, and to point the way to Him. The radical message demanded the authority of the One who had commissioned it. Paul said, "My message and my preaching were not with wise and persuasive words, but with a demonstration of the Spirit's power, so that your faith might not rest on men's wisdom, but on God's power."

The message of Christ is not only supernatural and miraculous at its core, but also timeless and unchanging. The message never changes – it Jesus Christ and Him crucified. The mandate of the Church is to preach the message of a powerful Jesus. The Church is not primarily about worship styles and ministries, about being cool and fitting in. At the heart of all we do must be the proclamation of Christ. We are seeking to reflect a 1st Century Jesus whilst expressing His desire to build a 21st Century Church that speaks an authentic message of salvation and the power of a new life.

The 1st Century church of the New Testament was all about Jesus, His mission and His message. The 21st Century Church needs to reflect this powerfully.

Christ is the message.

Who is this guy?

Since Jesus Christ is the beginning and the end, the very centre of our lives and message, let me close out this chapter by reminding us of *who Jesus really is* and all that He is and has done for us. If we are going to revolutionise our churches, we must start by revolutionising our lives as individuals, and that will happen as we are enraptured and captivated afresh by Christ.

Let's meet again the authentic and accessible Jesus, timeless and immortal, unforgettable – the One who desires to know us personally, who is utterly fascinated by us, loves us and possesses eternal power He wishes to share with us. He is rich in grace, abounding in mercy and abundant in favour towards us. This is a true picture of Jesus!

He stepped out of the timelessness of Heaven
He is begotten not created
He co-ruler of the universe with His Father and the Holy Spirit
He is co-creator of the heavens and the earth
He is co-creator of man and woman
Jesus is God, He is divine

He was referred to as Son of man and Son of God

He possessed the twin natures, being both fully God and fully man

And this is just the beginning!

He was born in a stable behind a hotel

He clothed Himself in human flesh, born as a man yet possessing the divine nature of God

He is sinless Himself, yet merciful to sinners

He is meek under provocation

He is dignified, yet without arrogance

He is pure Himself, yet with a deep insight into evil

He was accessible to the people of His day and never hid from people in need. He never misunderstood nor discouraged any sincere seeker.

The more closely you look at Jesus, the more He stands forth in peerless majesty and dignity. The closer you examine Him, the more you see the flawlessness of His divinity, the splendour of His humanity

Jesus was utterly void of resentment for wrongs, even wrongs against himself. "He was oppressed and afflicted, yet he did not open his mouth; he was led like a lamb to the slaughter, and as a sheep before her shearers is silent, so he did not open his mouth" (Isaiah 53:7). When apprehended, instead of sharing the disciples' indignation Jesus rebuked them; instead of condemning His murderers He prayed for them: "Father, forgive them, for they know not what they do" (Luke 23:34).

He was a champion to those who were downtrodden and embarrassed, such as the woman caught in adultery who was the recipient of His grace and compassion, not His judgement and condemnation.

He was strong, compassionate and caring. He was a real man who hung out with real guys, masculine, tough and intelligent.

He was fit and not afraid of hard work. Jesus was a true liberator of women and an affirmer of men. He loved children and sought to encourage them and bless them.

Jesus was a miracle worker; the impossible was His territory. He healed the blind, cured the lame, reached out to those who were sick and was willing to make well those whom society rejected – lepers and paralytic beggars.

Jesus moved in supernatural power by the Holy Spirit. He walked on water, turned water into wine, calmed a raging sea and spoke to wind to make it subside. He took a boy's lunch of two fish and five loaves and transformed it into a meal that fed thousands. He pulled money from a fish's mouth and cursed a fig tree so that it withered and died.

Jesus had authority over demons and even the devil himself was frustrated in his attempt to distract Him from His mission. With great authority Jesus cast out demons and set people free from the oppression of the devil. Jesus was unafraid; He was bold, fearless and undaunted by the powers of darkness. "Whenever the evil spirits saw him, they fell down before him and cried out, "You are the Son of God" (Mark 3:11)

Jesus delivered His teachings with authority. His messages were relevant, relatable and easy to grasp. His teachings were easy to apply to everyday life. His word was truth which set people free. People understood what He was saying and enjoyed listening to Him.

"The people were all so amazed that they asked each other, 'What is this? A new teaching – and with authority! He even gives orders to evil spirits and they obey Him.' News about him spread quickly over the whole region of Galilee." (Mark 1:27-28)

Jesus was authoritative, commanding and people followed Him. The men who became His disciples dropped what they were doing to follow Him. This confidence was transferred to the people of the 1st Century Church who were people so powerfully influenced by Him that they were willing to die for Him rather than deny Him.

Jesus was the supreme sacrifice of God for a sin-soaked world – the Lamb of God who came to take away the sins of the world. He is our Saviour and Redeemer. He has come to bring salvation, transformation and renewal to all who would believe in Him. He is the light of the world, the Bread of Life, the Good Shepherd who laid down His life for all, the Living Water given that whoever drinks of Him will never thirst again.

Jesus rose to life again so that we can experience His transforming love and walk in new life. He has risen, utterly defeating the powers of Satan and placing victory into the hands of all those who call up Christ's name.

This is no namby pamby Jesus, thin, emaciated and effeminate! He is Jesus, the Son of the Living God, Alpha and Omega, the beginning and the end, the First and the Last. He is Messiah, the Christ, the Anointed One of God who died and rose again from death, never to die again!

> He is alive to hear our every prayer and our every desperate thought
> He is alive to heal our heart and take from us the pains of a bitter world
> He is alive to forgive us of every sin
> He is alive to fill us with His power
> He is alive to help us find victory in our own personal battles with the devil and his legions from hell
> He is alive to inspire us with a destiny
> He is alive to anoint us with power
> He is the Christ, the Son of the Living God, who died but is now alive forever more
> He is alive forever more and He is planning His return to our world again – this time not as a suffering Saviour, but as King of Kings. He will return as promised in the Bible to

bring this world to its conclusion. He will come to wipe away all our tears and make everything new.

"For the Lord himself will come down from heaven, with a loud command, with the voice of the archangel and with the trumpet call of God, and the dead in Christ will rise first. After that, we who are still alive and are left will be caught up together with them in the clouds to meet the Lord in the air. And so we will be with the Lord forever. Therefore encourage each other with these words." (1 Thessalonians 4:14-18)

I present to you a 1st Century Christ for a 21st Century Church: powerful and strong, bold and ancient; able to deliver and able to care for you. This is the Jesus who is aware of your destiny and desires to work with you to achieve greatness in this life and eternity. This is Jesus who is able to forgive you of your sins, wash you clean and keep you clean. This is Jesus who is able to make you stand in His grace and walk under His favour! This is Jesus: strong, robust, unafraid of demons, powerful in the face of opposition. He is solid, durable and tough; no one can stand against Him. This is Jesus, Son of God, who confronted not only the devil but our last enemy, death itself. Jesus took back the sceptre of life and the keys of death and hell and was raised to new life by the Holy Spirit. Not even death could hold Him. This is a Christ who is mighty to save!
It is this Jesus who said,

"I will build my church, and the gates of Hades will not overcome it." (Matthew 16:18). Truly it will be a Church expansive with energy, passionate, vibrant, creative, innovative and original. A fresh and relevant Church. A 21st Century Church for today!

CONCLUSION

If we are going to build 21st Century churches then we need a bold, powerful and overwhelmingly fresh vision of Jesus – He who is first and last, head over everything for the Church.

> "He is the head of the body, the church; he is the beginning and the firstborn from among the dead, so that in everything he might have the supremacy. For God was pleased to have all his fullness dwell in him." (Colossians 1:18-19)

Paul writes in Ephesians 3:20-21,

> "Now to him who is able to do immeasurably more than all we ask or imagine, according to his power that is at work within us, to him be glory in the church and in Christ Jesus throughout all generations, forever and ever! Amen."

Amen! So be it. Let it happen Lord!

So, in summary:

We have discovered something is wrong in the Church and fixing the problem is complex, but we can find a solution. The first step in that solution is the restoration of anointed, godly leadership and a resolve to overcome the flawed structures of governance that are hindering the progress of so many churches.

Those leaders who want to "cross over" from where they were to where God wants them to be will need to be bold, courageous and uncompromising. They must determine to move forward empowered by the grace of Christ and the power of the Holy Spirit.

Together with God we must revisit the Master's plan as laid out in Scripture and work to make it a reality. We must become expert builders, working to God's blueprint.

Remember that God has a plan for the church in your city, town or village. The Church that is emerging is *confident, has a voice, is infused with God's presence, is victorious and should not be afraid to be BIG!*

Remember that the way you view the Church will determine the kind of local church you build with Him. If your vision is blurry, indistinct or off beam you will not build church according to the Master's plan. Remind yourself frequently of Christ's vision for His Church.

Remember that God designed the Church to be absolutely central to society. It is not peripheral and can never be sidelined. You are the most important institution in your town! God's plans and intentions for His world will only ever be fulfilled through the Church. God has no Plan B, no other vehicle He plans to work through.

The great challenge of the Church is to keep the main thing the main thing. We are easily diverted from our priority, so that we start doing all kinds of things that water down and dilute our presence in the world. We need to remind ourselves of the core mandate Jesus gave us: to go and make disciples of all nations.

We must be challenged on the question of who is building whose church! If we are not working to help Jesus build *His* Church then we are labouring in vain.

Part of our becoming a *relentless church* means a restoration of key values. We recall that:

God has chosen and sanctified His house
We need to recapture a sense of awe for the house of God
We need to release a new sense of energy in our churches
We need to teach people that in the Church is where they will truly connect with their own destiny and purpose
There are 7 key characteristics that sum up what a 21st Century relentless church looks like:
It is a place of revival
It is powerful and prophetic
It is salt and light to the world
It is in the world, but not of the world
It is a place of salvation
It is a spiritual house
It is culturally contemporary

Finally, we must recapture a true vision of the magnificence of our Lord Jesus Christ, for He is the centre, the beginning and end of all that we do.

Be encouraged by His words to Peter which hold true for us:

"Peter I have determined with gritty resolve to build my Church and it will be a powerful force – it will be so expansive with energy that even the designs of Hell will be unable to stop it, and guess what Peter? I will delight in using people just like you make my dream a reality!" (A personal paraphrase of Matthew 16:18)

"He who testifies to these things says, "Yes, I am coming soon." Amen. Come, Lord Jesus. The grace of the Lord Jesus be with God's people. Amen."
(Revelation 22:20-21)